A VISION IN WOOD & STONE

Palmer Hall, c.1992

A Vision in Wood & Stone

THE ARCHITECTURE OF MOUNT ALLISON UNIVERSITY

John Leroux & Thaddeus Holownia

GASPEREAU PRESS ꝗ PRINTERS AND PUBLISHERS 2016

This book is dedicated to the father-son teams of Charles A. Fowler & Charles A.E. Fowler, and F. Bruce Brown & Douglas Brown, Mount Allison's architects for almost sixty years.

Mount Allison, late 1890s

Foreword

Of the many types of artifacts that might record the story of a university—from official reports and archival documents to personal accounts—none capture an institution's development as directly and succinctly than its buildings. In this thoughtful study of the architecture of Mount Allison University, John Leroux and Thaddeus Holownia document the campus's evolution from a few wooden structures to its impressive present-day multiplicity of building materials and architectural styles. The story of these buildings speaks not only to the prosaic details of the institution's history, but also to the ambitious vision of excellence which motivated its founders and has guided the university's development over many generations. The authors also present the story of Mount Allison's campus within a wider social and aesthetic context, demonstrating not only its many qualities and physical beauty but also its bold embracement of, and occasional reaction against, global architectural movements such as Modernism. The process of designing and building a campus over many decades presents unique opportunities and challenges for a university. By examining both the physical structures and the rich complexity of human intention and action which animated their construction, this study serves to both expand our understanding of how Mount Allison's campus was formed and to sharpen our sense of responsibility for the quality of our built environment going forward, both on the campus and in the broader community.

ANDREW STEEVES, GASPEREAU PRESS

1.1 Mount Allison's Marjorie Young Bell Convocation Hall surrounded by Sackville in the foreground and the Tantramar Marsh in the background

CHAPTER ONE

A Classical Foundation

1839–1855

Before the great field, a temple emerges from the forest. Thaddeus Holownia's photograph of Mount Allison's Convocation Hall reaches right to the essence of this place—a richly layered landscape of beauty, history and consequence (Figure 1.1). Like Saul Steinberg's famous *New Yorker* cover that shows the world compressed at the edge of Manhattan, Holownia's bird's-eye view frames Sackville against a nearly infinite horizontal vista. It not only speaks to this stone structure basking in the sun, it captures its neighbouring community, the natural terrain and their connection to the world beyond. The photograph reveals a place that was once an industrial hub of eastern Canada, bordering a stretch some called the "world's largest hayfield," where thin vertical wisps of the CBC Radio International towers once connected us to the rest of the planet. Further back, this very ground witnessed the European fight for control of Acadia. Even further back, the Mi'kmaq named the district Siknikt (where the Chignecto Isthmus got its name). The land here is resonant of nature and humanity.

But to many, the strongest connection to the region is what lies at the centre of the panoramic image; it is home to Mount Allison University, one of the most revered and beautiful educational environments in Canada. For 175 years the aspirational character of the university and its preceding schools has been captured in its architecture, a point that has not been acknowledged nearly enough in their long history. The architecture of Mount Allison chronicles the values and vision that built this place. Its venerable buildings, spaces and public art speak to a remarkable purpose and creative vision.

Unlike New Brunswick's three other public universities (University of New Brunswick, St. Thomas University and l'Université de Moncton) which retain virtually every building ever constructed, Mount Allison has fundamentally rebuilt and reinvented itself architecturally many times since its birth. Some of these instances have been by choice, while others have been forced upon it by fate. More than a linear history of construction in a distinct part of Canada, Mount Allison is a powerful architectural barometer: a fascinating tale of fashion, fires and fundraising, constantly tempered by the spirit of the times.

The first significant European settlement in present-day southeastern New Brunswick arose in the early 1670s, when a group of French Acadian families wanted to take advantage of the vast expanse of marshland and leave the instability of the Port Royal settlement across the Bay of Fundy. Small communities began to take shape on the Tantramar Marsh, an area they called Beaubassin ("fine river basin").

The Acadians were essentially left alone by the colonial powers to cultivate the rich tidal marshes which were some of the most productive farmland in coastal North America. Their livelihoods harmonized with their environment as they exploited the saturated land through an ingenious system of aboiteau dykes that drained many of the fields that are still farmed to this day. It was a masterful fusion of landscape, creative ingenuity and construction. By the mid eighteenth century, most Acadians in the territory were working on the marshlands. The terrain was fertile and picturesque, but ultimately too valuable and strategic to remain uncontested.

In the 1750s, mistrust and animosity between the French and the English empires grew so serious that war broke out. The French military's Beaubassin stronghold, Fort Beauséjour, fell in a matter of days, and the Acadians who refused to swear allegiance to the conquering British King were brutally deported. By the 1760s a small group of American settlers claimed the abandoned land, and the Township of Sackville began. Between 1772 and 1775 more than a thousand immigrants from Yorkshire crossed the ocean to join them. In time, Sackville became an important community that boasted productive farms, thriving factories and shipbuilding wharves along the muddy Tantramar River (Figure 1.2). Sackville also became a regional stronghold of Methodist religion, with many of the original Yorkshire settlers sharing this conviction.

Around 1816, a young Charles Frederick Allison (1795–1858) moved from Nova Scotia to Sackville to join the growing mercantile business run by his cousin William Crane and Bardin Turner. Within a few years he became a partner. Allison and

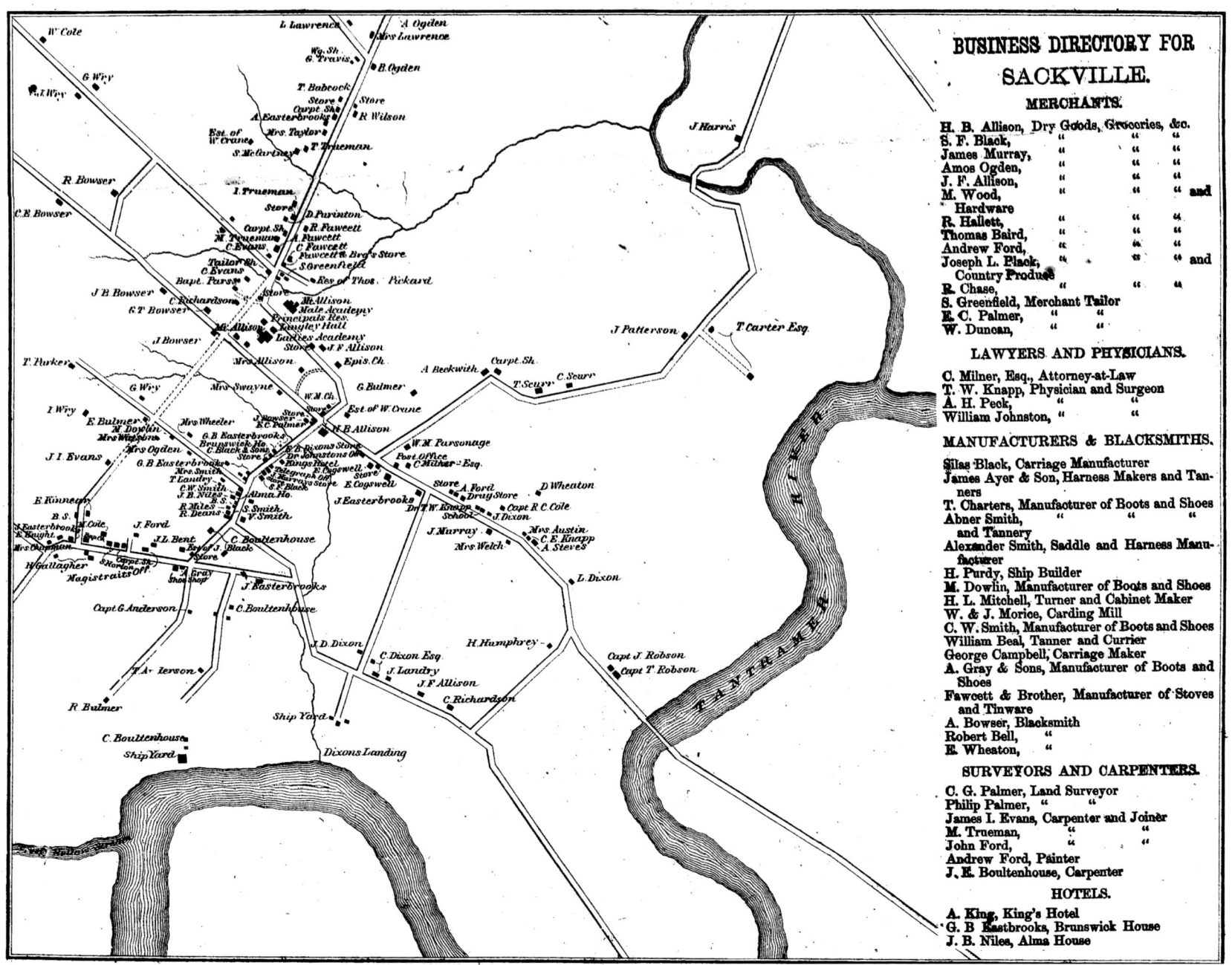

BUSINESS DIRECTORY FOR SACKVILLE.

MERCHANTS.

H. B. Allison, Dry Goods, Groceries, &c.
S. F. Black,   "   "   "
James Murray,   "   "   "
Amos Ogden,   "   "   "
J. F. Allison,   "   "   "
M. Wood,   "   "   " and
    Hardware
R. Hallett,   "   "   "
Thomas Baird,   "   "   "
Andrew Ford,   "   "   "
Joseph L. Black,   "   "   " and
    Country Produce
R. Chase,   "   "   "
S. Greenfield, Merchant Tailor
E. C. Palmer,   "   "
W. Duncan,   "   "

LAWYERS AND PHYSICIANS.

C. Milner, Esq., Attorney-at-Law
T. W. Knapp, Physician and Surgeon
A. H. Peck,   "   "
William Johnston,   "   "

MANUFACTURERS & BLACKSMITHS.

Silas Black, Carriage Manufacturer
James Ayer & Son, Harness Makers and Tanners
T. Charters, Manufacturer of Boots and Shoes
Abner Smith,   "   "   "
    and Tannery
Alexander Smith, Saddle and Harness Manufacturer
H. Purdy, Ship Builder
M. Dowlin, Manufacturer of Boots and Shoes
H. L. Mitchell, Turner and Cabinet Maker
W. & J. Morice, Carding Mill
C. W. Smith, Manufacturer of Boots and Shoes
William Beal, Tanner and Currier
George Campbell, Carriage Maker
A. Gray & Sons, Manufacturer of Boots and
    Shoes
Fawcett & Brother, Manufacturer of Stoves
    and Tinware
A. Bowser, Blacksmith
Robert Bell,   "
E. Wheaton,   "

SURVEYORS AND CARPENTERS.

C. G. Palmer, Land Surveyor
Philip Palmer,   "
James I. Evans, Carpenter and Joiner
M. Trueman,   "   "
John Ford,   "   "
Andrew Ford, Painter
J. E. Boultenhouse, Carpenter

HOTELS.

A. King, King's Hotel
G. B. Eastbrooks, Brunswick House
J. B. Niles, Alma House

1.2 1862 map and business directory of Sackville with Mount Allison at the upper left. From the H.F. Walling map of Albert and Westmorland counties

16

1. Letter from C.F Allison to W. Temple, June 4, 1839. [WMMS, box 101, file IIb, no. 14]

2. Letter from Enoch Wood to *The Wesleyan* (Halifax), May 19, 1882.

Crane became extremely prosperous as distributors of local produce and imported goods, as well as exporters of timber to Great Britain. As Crane became more and more active in provincial politics, management of the firm's affairs fell to Allison, who became admired as a cautious but shrewd businessman.

Born and raised Anglican, Allison began to attend local Methodist services in 1833 and was converted by 1836. The Methodists had long hoped to open an affiliated educational institution in the Maritimes but were unable to raise the funds. They now had a dedicated and financially skilled champion on their side. In early June of 1839, Allison proposed to the Wesleyan Methodists that a preparatory school for boys be established in Sackville where "not only the Elementary but higher branches of Education may be taught."[1] His proposal was timely, as around this time a number of Maritime schools with religious ties were founded, including St. Mary's in Halifax (Catholic) and Acadia in Wolfville (Baptist). Kings College in Fredericton (later the University of New Brunswick) was strongly connected to the Church of England and was considered by many as being geared to the upper class. A Methodist institution was seen by some as being a balancing spiritual force in the region. Allison offered to buy the land, pay for the necessary building and donate £100 annually for its first 10 years of operation. It was a generous offer indeed, but one that still had to weave through the proper channels to gain approval.

The church leaders were persuaded through the dialogue of local meetings, followed by discussions with Methodist ministers in Saint John. Allison's dream was finally accepted at a joint meeting of the New Brunswick and Nova Scotia Methodist districts in Halifax on July 12, 1839. A subsequent letter from attendee Reverend Enoch Wood vividly recalled Allison's presentation:

One would have thought by his unassumed humility that he came there to ask some special favor, rather than to make a noble and generous offer for the benefit of others. One sentence of his address I have never forgotten ...—"The Lord hath put it into my heart to give this sum towards building a Wesleyan Academy," —and then he made a short pause, as though he was afraid he had spoken too strongly, resuming —"I know the impression is from the Lord, for I am naturally fond of money."[2]

A comfortable life now in hand, Allison wanted to ensure that his educational dream became a reality, so he retired from his lucrative business by January 1840 and focused all of his energy towards establishing the new school—appropriately named the Mount Allison Wesleyan Academy. The institution's intent was now fully supported, so the physical work had to begin. As with any new project, three things were needed to get the building up and running: a program, a site and an architect/builder team. The first requirement was fairly straightforward, and fortunately for Allison and the future academy, the latter two were achieved brilliantly.

It would be difficult to imagine Sackville today without the Mount Allison campus perched atop its small hill overlooking the town, but when Allison purchased the land it was largely unoccupied. The five-acre site was bought from Christopher Atkinson, the son of one of the Yorkshire settlers who had acquired it from one of the original 1760s American immigrants. In contention, some suggested that the new school should be located in the bustling port of Saint John and not the small town of Sackville. Allison insisted that the school was to serve all the Maritimes, not just New Brunswick, and so the Sackville location was crucial. With this wider focus in mind, Allison would have surely been pleased as the subsequent university would later claim a truly international sphere of influence. Besides, there was a precedent for Methodist educational institutions locating in smaller centres, away from the 'distractions' of the large cities.

The site was established at the edge of the town, about where present-day Campbell Hall stands. At a planning committee meeting on January 17, 1840, Allison announced his intention to spend £4000 on the building's construction—described by Enoch Wood as "a very auspicious beginning."[3] The architect selected was a young man named Samuel C. Bugbee of Saint John. Little known in the accounts of Canadian architectural history, Bugbee would go on to become a renowned architect in the United States. Born in St. Stephen in 1812, Bugbee trained as a house carpenter and at an early age showed great promise as a man of substantial design talent. Before winning the commission to design the Mount Allison Academy building, he had assisted with the design and construction of Centenary Methodist Church in Saint John in 1838 under the guidance of architect John Cunningham.

Several years after completing the Mount Allison Academy building, Bugbee moved to Boston where he established a successful architectural practice designing houses and hotels. His greatest professional success, however, would come after

3. Letter from Enoch Wood to secretaries of Wesleyan missions, January 24, 1840. [WMMS, box 101, file IIb, no. 42]

4. "Death of a Former Resident of St. Andrews," in *Saint John Daily Telegraph* (September 21, 1877).

5. Letter from Enoch Wood to secretaries of Wesleyan missions, January 24, 1840. [WMMS, box 101, file IIb, no. 42]

6. *British North American Wesleyan Methodist Magazine* (July 1842), p. 274.

7. Letter from W.M. Leggett to 'Mr. McCausland,' July 26, 1842. [MAA, 8123]

1.3 Leland Stanford house, San Francisco (Samuel C. Bugbee, 1876)

he moved to San Francisco in 1861, where he established an office with his son, Charles, and designed such grand commissions as the California Theatre, Mills Hall, Union Hall and lavish mansions for such families as the Stanfords, of Stanford University fame (Figure 1.3). He even served as a member of the California State Legislature in 1866–67. Bugbee's Sackville project was certainly the stepping stone that gave him the confidence and patronage to make his way southward, establishing a lineage connecting the architecture of Mount Allison to a number of major American monuments. Samuel C. Bugbee died in Oakland, California, in 1877, with his obituary affirming that "no man stood higher in his profession."[4]

Informed by travels in the United States where Bugbee gathered information on similar buildings, his design for the academy building was fully approved by Allison except for a decorative rooftop tower that was eliminated for cost reasons, along with it being considered too ornate for a Methodist institution. This bit of restraint was echoed by Enoch Wood, who stated that the building was to embrace "respectability and comfort, blended with economy."[5] While one would expect a rather restrained and humble structure from this statement, the building was an excellent instance of Neoclassical design and one of the more refined examples of the style in Eastern Canada. This was all the more noteworthy as it was the creation of a relatively untested young architect.

Allison laid the cornerstone for the Mount Allison Wesleyan Academy on July 9, 1840, and would personally supervise the construction. By the summer of 1841, the building's exterior was completed, and a year later an article in the *British North American Wesleyan Methodist Magazine* reported that the building was "probably unsurpassed by any wooden fabric, erected for similar purposes, on the American continent."[6] Heavy praise, tempered by a private letter of 1842 that stated a bit more moderately "our new Academy at Sackville … is a noble structure,—superb, but plain & truly Methodistical."[7] While it is not easy to grasp exactly what that last adjective meant, the general sentiment is fitting. Methodist in beliefs and curriculum, it was important to note that the school was still open to students of other denominations.

A building that would have appeared palatial compared to the rest of the town, the academy was 150-feet long, 45-feet wide and four-storeys tall, with the bottom floor/basement being set partially below grade. A superb daguerreotype of the original building still survives (Figure 1.4). An ell wing pushed out from the rear,

1.4 Circa 1843 daguerreotype of the Mount Allison Wesleyan Academy (Samuel C. Bugbee, 1843), the first academy building

8. Leslie Maitland, *Neoclassical Architecture in Canada* (Ottawa: Parks Canada, 1984), p. 11.

making an overall T-shape for the edifice. The symmetrical main facade was centred around a grand portico with a huge triangular pediment roof set above an entablature and four Doric columns that stood like sentinels atop the wide entry stair. Trying to emulate end-pavillions while being mindful of the project finances, Bugbee designed a largely Greek Revival treatment at the extremities of the main facade. Their flat Classical pilasters "holding up" smooth lintels below the roof edge give weight and framed balance to the extended front of gridded windows. The whole composition was set under a low sloping gable roof that ran parallel to the street. A material choice that was convenient for its local availability and strength was the red sandstone for the foundation—a distinct selection that, unbeknownst to Allison and Bugbee, would one day be almost the official cladding for nearly all of Mount Allison's architecture.

While the builders had little choice but to use wood for its skin rather than the more expensive and laborsome stone, it still had a tremendous weight and robustness. It was simple, yet monumental. While the Neoclassical style was in vogue at the time, there is little doubt that the choice of a large white Classical building with enormous columns atop a hill was a tipping of the hat to the Acropolis in Athens and its evocation of higher ideals, democracy and a strong classical education. The design could not have been more deliberate. It tied tiny Sackville to the rest of Western civilization. As historian Leslie Maitland recounts in *Neoclassical Architecture in Canada*:

Neoclassicism was a pan-cultural, pan-national current, growing out of a new examination of the past, and of the natural world. It produced trends in thought and fashion that were to affect all of the arts, literature, dress, manners, decorative arts, and of course the architecture, of Western society. Neoclassicism began as a rational, eighteenth century analysis of history and nature seeking the underlying universal laws pointing the way towards a harmonious existence for mankind.[8]

At the time, historicism and a fervent reaching back to the past were not seen as derivative or merely copying, they were considered an entirely appropriate way to frame the buildings of the era. Robert Adam (1728–1792), the influential Scottish architect, stated that "The buildings of the Ancients are in Architecture, what the works of Nature are with respect to the other Arts; they serve as models which we should imitate, and as standards by which we ought to judge."[9]

The positive imprint that the soon-to-be Mount Allison placed on its young Saint John architect was clear. Life in Sackville seemed equally buoyant. In a letter that he wrote to Charles Allison on September 29, 1842, Samuel Bugbee reflected that:

I was very happy to hear from you and to hear from my Brother that the Academy is about going in to operation and I hope it will more than meet your expectations. I feel a very great interest in it and must say that I feel more attached to Sackville than any place I ever was in and it's the same with Mrs. B[ugbee].[10]

By the time the building opened to students on January 19, 1843, it was half a year late and cost double Allison's initial £4000 budget, but was greatly admired. It was completely furnished and equipped with "Chemical, philosophical and Astronomical apparatus"[11] and had a rudimentary library. A school inspector's report from November 1844 relayed that "The interior arrangements of the building are excellent, not only for the purposes of instruction, but also for the comfort and accommodation of the Students as a home or place of residence during the continuance of their studies."[12] The building lodged professors and a steward, apartments for the principal and governor at each end of the main wing, a large lecture hall, two classrooms, a library and study space, a dining room and kitchen in the basement, and 40 rooms that could hold up to four students each. In the colder months, the academy was heated by any number of stoves that were fuelled by student-chopped firewood, one of their required regular duties.

Like the building, the new school was sound. Critical to its success was the appointment of Rev. Humphrey Pickard as principal—a young Methodist minister from New Brunswick who atypically had a university degree. Pickard had strong experiences in education and business, as well as the Methodist ministry, and he proved a capable and trustworthy leader, serving for 26 years.

As one would expect in the mid-nineteenth-century male-dominated society, the Mount Allison Wesleyan Academy was a male-only school when it opened for business, but not for long. In a welcoming spirit of conciliation, a major change was proposed in July 1847 at a meeting in Sackville of the New Brunswick and Nova

9. Robert Adam, *Ruins of the Palace of the Emperor Diocletian at Spalatro in Dalmatia* (London: Robert Adam, 1764), p. 1.

10. Letter from Samuel Bugbee to Charles Allison, September 29, 1842. [MAA, 7946, Scrapbook 3, 22/1]

11. Letter from William Temple and Sampson Busby (trustees of the Wesleyan Academy) to the Lieutenant-Governor, Legislative Council and Assembly of New Brunswick, February 16, 1843. [PANB, RG2, RS8, group I, I/4]

12. "Report from J. Brown, Esquire, on Wesleyan Academy, Sackville," in *Journal of the House of Assembly of the Province of New Brunswick, from the twenty ninth day of January, to the fourteenth day of April, 1845* (Fredericton: John Simpson [printer], 1845), pp. ciii–civ.

13. *Minutes of New Brunswick District* (July 3, 1847), pp. 425–6. [MCA]

14. *Mount Allison Academic Gazette* (December 1853), p. 7. [MAA]

15. Letter from James Robert Inch (Principal, Mount Allison Ladies' Academy, 1869–78) in *The Chignecto Post & Borderer*, June 3, 1880. Cited in John Reid, "The Education of Women at Mount Allison," in *Acadiensis* (Spring 1983), p. 19.

16. Raymond Clare Archibald, *Historical Notes on the Education of Women at Mount Allison 1854–1954* (Sackville: Centennial Committee, Mount Allison University, 1954), p. 1.

17. *Mount Allison Academic Gazette* (December 1854), pp. 2–4. [MAA]

18. *Mount Allison Academic Gazette* (June 1854), p. 7. [MAA]

Scotia Methodist districts. They passed a resolution in favour of "the necessity and desirableness of establishing an Institution under the controal [*sic*] of our Church similar to that we have in the case of the Sackville Academy for the religious education of Females."[13] Principal Pickard was given the task of investigating the plan.

This goal took time to bear fruit. The years 1848–50 were beset by an economic depression that caused a steep decline in enrollment. The academy became set on more solid legal ground when it was officially incorporated by the provincial legislature in April 1849. By the recovery of the early 1850s, Maritime-wide fundraising efforts were becoming more and more successful and things were looking much better for the needed expansion. In December 1853 the plan was made public. Course descriptions and regulations for the new female branch of the academy were unveiled, and it was announced that its "commodious and beautiful edifice"[14] was close to being completed. A multi-building campus was born, one that "boldly opened its doors to all irrespective of sex."[15]

Slightly more unassuming than the male academy building, the female academy was situated just inside where the present Bell Library/Crabtree colonnade stands. The three-storey wooden building had a low hip roof capped by a small cupola at the centre (Figure 1.5). Its 11-bay facade was similar to the detailing of the male academy building through its window arrangement, clapboard siding and wide Neoclassical corner boards. A single-storey portico framed the main entry with four columns supporting a small balustrade. The edifice was sometimes called the 'White House', as it had always been painted white, save for a short period in 1896 when it was a criticized (and quickly overpainted) "sombre brown."[16]

The female academy building was designed to accommodate 70 student boarders within its rectangular plan. However, it proved to be so popular after its official opening on August 17, 1854, that its first term numbers reached an enrollment of 118—6 more students than the male school. This was nothing but good news as principal Pickard called it "an auspicious beginning of the new epoch."[17] The June 1854 issue of the *Mount Allison Academic Gazette* claimed in no uncertain terms that the female academy building was "designed to be in every respect, in proportion to its extent, equal to any public Institution devoted to the advancement of Female Education on the Continent."[18] The exterior grounds were equally important, with the rear yard being a perfect spot for barns and outbuildings, while the front lawn plateau was used for social gatherings and "Physical Culture" drills (Figure 1.6).

1.5 Sketch of the original building for the female branch of the Mount Allison Wesleyan Academy, 1854

1.6 The female academy's front lawn plateau, showing a crowd gathered for their "physical culture" drills

19. *New Brunswick Assembly Journal* (1854), p. 223.

20. *Mount Allison Academic Gazette* (June 1854), p. 7. [MAA]

21. *Mount Allison Academic Gazette* (December 1853), p. 7. [MAA]

Through its continued success and growth, the female academy soon became almost unrecognizable from its original shape. It was altered and expanded no less than five times over the next 117 years, before it was demolished in 1971.

Although a clear distinction and inevitable rivalry would be maintained for many years between the allied academy branches, the curriculum of the female academy would inspire in no small part the future academic direction of Mount Allison University. While the boys' school concentrated on a classical/liberal education supplemented by scientific and technical courses, the female curriculum was similarly rigorous but also stressed "French and other polite Languages, Music, Drawing, Painting, and other ornamental Branches"[19] as well as the cultivation of "refined taste and lady-like manners"[20] through residence life. With expansive energy and growing numbers, the stage was now set for a major architectural evolution that would benefit those on both sides of the separating road, a lane appropriately christened as the "Academy Stretch."

To this effect, the *Mount Allison Academic Gazette* printed an article giving notice that:

The erection of the Academy for Females, and the proposed consequent enlargement of Educational operations at Mount Allison, have rendered it exceedingly desirable, nay indispensable, if these operations are to be carried on comfortably, that another Building should be provided, to contain a large Lecture Room or Chapel, and suitable apartments for Library, Museum &c.

We are sure that the announcement which we are now authorized to make will exceedingly gratify all the numerous friends of the Institution. A noble-minded friend of Education has undertaken to provide for the erection of such a Building at his own sole expense.[21]

On January 30, 1855, the expansive 'New Hall' located to the north beside the female academy building was dedicated (Figure 1.7). Admission tickets to the day's events cost five shillings each. Featuring a great auditorium with a steeply sloping floor, a gallery over the main entrance and curved rear walls behind the elevated stage, it could seat 700 as well as boast a library and space for a small scientific museum. In 1857, a massive pipe organ specially built in Massachusetts for the hall was installed facing the audience (Figure 1.8). The elegant building (on the site

1.7 'New Hall'/Lingley Hall, 1855

1.8 Interior view of the 'New Hall'/Lingley Hall, showing the pipe organ at the rear of the stage

22. *Provincial Wesleyan* (February 15, 1855).

23. *Mount Allison Academic Gazette* (December 1854), p. 4. [MAA]

where Hart Hall now stands) provided the allied schools a proper space for large lectures, concerts and convocations. It was also remembered as one of the few locations where the schools' girls and boys gathered together in any organized way; a key point for the student bodies that now boasted a combined count of just under 300.

Overlooking the town below, the hall's main facade was a crowning achievement for the hill site: a Roman temple-like structure with an Ionic front that created a bold, heroic presence aside its hip-roofed neighbour. The DNA of Mount Allison's campus was beginning to form: a series of elegant buildings on a modest rise, a focal point on the landscape with their varied architectural expressions that were aligned yet individualistic, and all exceedingly conscious of the open spaces and physical connections between.

The hall can actually be labelled *tetrastyle in antis*, a formal phrase used to describe ancient Classical temples that have four (tetra) columns on the front between *antae*, which were the rectangular column-like piers formed at the end of the side walls. The venerable arrangement created a welcome covered porch for those entering or leaving the building, as well as a favourite location for group photos along its wide front steps (Figure 1.9). Charles Allison once again introduced Pickard at the hall's opening, who spoke at length on what the school had achieved over the past decade and more. Pickard realized the great achievement of the academy's female branch, and especially that this new building was "so much needed for the effective and comfortable working of the united Institution." He concluded by trumpeting that the new hall should long stand as "a temple sacred to literature, science and religion combined!"[22] The dedication ceremony was followed by two parallel teas—males in one building and females in another—with everyone reconvening in the hall for an evening "enlivened with Music and Scientific Experiments of an interesting character."[23]

An even more purist Classical structure than the male academy building, the architectural form of the new hall (soon to be named Lingley Hall) was, as Pickard so enthusiastically pointed out, very much a temple that was broad in its reach and tenure. Its architectural design spoke not only to its physical scale and scholastic values, but to the very nature of what the academies were about. It would also have an enormous impact on the design of Mount Allison buildings right up to the present. The great colonnaded faces of the current Convocation Hall and

1.9 Group photo at the front steps of Lingley Hall, c.1885

1.10 Mount Allison, 1862: (L to R) The female academy's gymnasium, service barns, the female academy building, Lingley Hall and the male academy building its kindred predecessor, Fawcett Hall, are indebted in their appearance to this initial auditorium building built for those young men and women back in the mid nineteenth century.

That same year a small gymnasium was built next to the female academy building to ensure their physical health via "a regular course of Calisthenics, comprehending all the movements required to develop every part of the muscular frame ..."[24] Little is known about this modest building except through early photographs. It appears to be an almost residential five-bay structure with a central door along its long facade (Figure 1.10). In 1892, the gymnasium was moved behind the adjacent female academy building (now known as the Mount Allison Wesleyan Ladies' College) and became the ladies' college dining hall in January 1893. It was subsequently refitted as the Lillian Massey-Treble School of Household Science in 1904. One of the oldest remaining buildings on campus, it was demolished in 1971.

By the end of 1855, Charles Allison's vision had been amply realized, although in the coming years it would only continue to grow, both in size and in architectural accomplishment. From today's vantage point, every single Mount Allison building mentioned in this chapter is long gone, but their influence and effect were enormous. The dream of the campus becoming a well-established member of the Sackville community took hold through its architecture, where the development of young students was physically and symbolically connected to their surroundings. Over the coming decades, structures would be enlarged, altered and added, while materials would become more robust and ornately considered. But the white clapboarded wooden Mount Allison that sheltered and inspired the initial cohorts was created with care and craftsmanship—a foundational sensibility that would remain with the campus for the rest of its life.

24. *Mount Allison Academic Gazette* (December 1855), p. 6. [MAA]

CHAPTER TWO

Shaping an Academic Acropolis
1855–1900

As the Mount Allison campus grew, the need arose for a proper residence for its headmaster. In 1857 a designated house was built between the male and female academies for Principal (and later President) Humphrey Pickard and his successors (Figure 2.1). It was a refined one-and-a-half storey Greek Revival cottage with some Gothic Revival touches, although its roof was raised and a two-storey bay window added in 1903, giving the house its present appearance (Figure 2.2). It is still known as the President's Cottage, although university presidents have not occupied it since 1957. The house was considered for demolition in 1965, but was saved from the wrecking ball and restored as a centennial project at a time when the university was fast ridding itself of its historic wooden architecture. According to the university's own report, the President's Cottage would "be the only [building] to remain to mark the early days of Mount Allison" and "when restored to some semblance of its former graceful appearance it should again take its place in the life of the University."[1] Since then it has served as an overflow student residence, faculty housing, academic building and in its present role as the University Club/ Dining Room.

The year 1858 was a busy one for the school. Its college charter was granted by the New Brunswick Legislature and given the Lieutenant-Governor's assent on April 6, 1858. It was also the year that the force behind the very existence of Mount Allison passed away. Charles Allison died on November 20, 1858, and his funeral was held in a packed Lingley Hall. The air was filled with mourning and praise for the man the *Provincial Wesleyan* described as "a benefactor to his race, a blessing to his country, an ornament to the age in which he lived."[2] Fortunately for Mount Allison, the close of the Charles Allison era would in no way end his vision.

1. *Mount Allison University Centennial Project Report.* [MAA 8326/11/78]

2. *Provincial Wesleyan* (November 25, 1858).

2.1 President's Cottage, 1857

3. Letter from John Allison to Leonard Tilley, December 26, 1860. [PANB, RG4, RS24/861/re/I]

4. Quoted in Walter Donlan, *The Aristocratic Ideal and Selected Papers* (Wauconda, IL: Bolchazy-Carducci, 1999), p. 125.

A problem that every college or private school wants to contend with is constantly increasing enrollment. The female branch of the Mount Allison Wesleyan Academy had 153 girls attend in 1858–59, and a mere one year later the number remarkably rose to 189, rendering the facilities "uncomfortably crowded."[3] As a result, six years following its opening a north wing was added to the female academy building for the princely cost of £600. Under a gable roof that was perpendicular to the main building, the new wing provided space for another 40 boarders, as well as classrooms, music rooms, art rooms and an expanded dining hall. By now the gathering of white buildings atop the Mount Allison hill would have pleased the ancient Greeks, who not only considered the interrelationship of structures to their site as crucial, but that their beauty was a virtue (Figure 1.10). As the Athenian statesman Pericles claimed in his famous funeral oration of 430 BC: "Our love of what is beautiful does not lead to extravagance; our love of the things of the mind does not make us soft."[4] Responding to continued growth, by 1875 a matching wing would be added to the southern end of the female academy building, along with a new mansard roof above the entire structure, giving it a full extra storey of greatly needed space (Figure 2.3).

In 1855, Mount Allison was an institution with two aligned academy schools. By July 1862 the degree-granting Mount Allison Wesleyan College opened, with its first two students graduating with bachelor of arts degrees in May 1863. With this maturing came yet another new building, College Hall, the first one entirely devoted to the college proper (Figure 2.4). Formally opened on New Year's Day 1863, it stood to the northwest of the President's Cottage, with a white wooden exterior like its neighbours. Through an unpretentious form not unlike the original female academy building with its three-storey hip-roofed design and small cupola, the 68-feet by 40-feet structure housed a lecture room, library, four classrooms on the ground floor, a large students' meeting room and 16 individual study rooms on the upper two floors. College Hall would be recurrently altered and renamed: a portico was added in 1871–72 (Figure 2.5); the building was moved in 1883 and converted to a student residence; it was raised and renovated in 1903 to become a science building; again fully renovated and refinished on the outside in 1921; added to in 1925 and 1927; and then finally succumbing to fire in March 1933. Gathering no moss, College Hall's future names included: the Lodge, Old

2.2 The present-day President's Cottage, showing the upper storey addition

2.3 The ladies' academy building showing the new southern wing and mansard roof storey above, c.1886

2.4 The town of Sackville with Mount Allison in the background, c.1863. College Hall is under construction at the centre of the image immediately to the right of Lingley Hall

Lodge, McClelan School of Applied Science, Science Hall, Science Building and, finally, the Old Science Building.

5. *Mount Allison Academy and Commercial College Calendar* (1933–34), p. 61. [MAA]

But as previously mentioned, Mount Allison would never simply be a slow accretion of buildings. As one was added, another could inevitably be taken away by accident. On January 16, 1866, a tragic event took place that shattered the first male academy building, an episode that would persistently strike every decade or so for the next 75 years, claiming substantial extents of Mount Allison: fire.

Allegedly started by the boiling over of a kettle of fat, the fire began just before 6:00 PM, and within a few hours the building was completely destroyed. A replacement structure being desperately needed, donations rolled in from around the Maritimes, Newfoundland and even Bermuda. Rebuilding began in haste. The new building rose "phoenix-like from the ashes of its predecessor,"[5] with its cornerstone being laid on May 15, 1866. The architect's name was Rev. George Butcher, although little is known about him or his work. The second male academy building was essentially the same size and volume as its razed ancestor, although it was of a different architectural style: the then fashionable Italianate. Decisively different from the Neoclassical and Gothic Revival buildings of the day, Italianate architecture derived from the palazzos of the Italian Renaissance and subsequent Mannerist buildings. North American Italianate structures were typically known for their overall square massing, shallow hip roofs with cupolas, decorated eaves and brackets, and slender windows (often arched). The second male academy building fit the category perfectly.

While little of its recorded history can be found, photographs and engravings show it as a handsome wooden building with a long hip roof, arched recesses along the facades and a similar spatial approach as the original. Reflecting its projecting central frontispiece and balustrade, the ends had ever-so-slightly raised "pavilions" pushing out from the corners (Figure 2.6). No Italianate building of the era was complete unless it had a prominent cupola, and this new structure was no exception. Where the 1843 academy's cupola was cautiously omitted, the new building proudly sported its four-sided lantern, featuring a low slope hipped roof, pairs of arch-top windows on each face and a decorative surface that matched the rest of the exterior. The official opening was on August 8, 1867, an auspicious day for many, as only a month previous, Canada had been born as a nation.

The institution had another exceptional year in 1875, as it saw Mount Allison

2.5 College Hall after its new front portico was added

2.6 The second building housing the male branch of the Mount Allison Wesleyan Academy (Rev. George Butcher, 1867)

Wesleyan College confer a degree to Grace Annie Lockhart, the first woman to earn a bachelor's degree in the British Empire. The year before, the Mount Allison Commercial College for men was established, and in 1875 construction began on a three-storey mansard-roofed building to house it beside the second male academy building. Initially built for $5000, the Commercial College would later be expanded, moved and connected with the next iteration of the male academy, as fire made its initial setting short-lived.

In 1882, the academy's student newspaper, *The Argosy*, reported the "second sacrifice to the fire-Fiend, at Mount Allison."[6] On January 8, fire started at the northern end of the second male academy building's kitchen from an overheated furnace, and slowly spread through the rest of the structure. *The Argosy* noted that "By daylight on Sunday morning the building was laid in ashes, and nothing but broken chimneys and crumbling walls remained to tell where stood the commodious Halls in which so many youths of the Maritime Provinces had lived and learned." The Commercial College, which stood only a few dozen feet from the blaze, was apparently saved "by means of wet carpets spread over the side, and other timely precautions."[7] The young males, now homeless, were allowed to temporarily dine at the Mount Allison Ladies' Academy, which understandably caused somewhat of a commotion in the routine.

And so the agenda of 16 years previous started from scratch once again. Fortunately the building had been insured for $16,000, and this covered most of the cost of its replacement. The new academy (the third on the same site) saw its cornerstone laid on a cold and wet June 5, 1882, by wealthy Sackville businessman and Mount Allison treasurer Josiah Wood "as they sang a solemn hymn and prayed."[8] Officially opened on January 4, 1883, the replacement building (Figures 2.7, 2.8) was designed by the distinguished architect G. Ernest Fairweather of Saint John, whose other buildings included St. Bernard's Catholic Church in Moncton, Saint John High School, the Saint John Public Library, and the University of New Brunswick Science/Engineering building. It was built by "Dorchester's Master Builder,"[9] John Teed, the same contractor who would oversee a number of prominent Mount Allison projects such as Centennial Hall and the Owens Art Gallery.

The new 145-feet long male academy building was taller than its predecessors, standing at four full storeys above a finished basement. Taking every precaution,

6. *The Argosy* (January 1882), p. 42. [MAA]

7. *The Argosy* (January 1882), p. 42. [MAA]

8. Diary of Laura S. Wood, 'Journal of Everyday Affairs', p. 34.

9. Helen M. Petchy, *Dorchester's Master Builder, John Francis Teed* (Dorchester, NB: Westmorland Historical Society, 1989).

2.7 The third male academy building, Mount Allison Wesleyan Academy (G. Ernest Fairweather, 1883)

the ovens and kitchen were designed so that "they shall have no contact with any wood work."[10] Noteworthy were its technical advances, such as a hot water heating system and contemporary plumbing. The building was designed once again in the popular architectural fashion of the day, which was now the Second Empire style.

In vogue from 1870 to around 1885, Second Empire buildings are distinguished by their rich sculptural ornamentation and prominent mansard roof, a roof with two slopes on all four sides. The steeply-sloped lower roof usually incorporates decorated dormer windows and ornate brackets at the junction of the wall and roof, while the upper roof is shallow and sometimes out of view. Buildings tend to be symmetrical and squarish, often featuring central projecting towers with a mansard roof and wrought iron cresting around the top.

Architectural progress and fresh economic wealth were changing the Mount Allison landscape. The academy building and its adjacent commercial appendage were perfect examples, as they seemed to morph at every other glance (Figures 2.9, 2.10). Across the road, the existing College Hall was now too small and in poor condition, so Josiah Wood promised to donate $10,000 towards the construction of a new college building if another $50,000 could be raised. The board agreed, and soon a pristine academic facility would appear; one that would have a profound and lasting effect on the future architectural path of Mount Allison. Rather than being clad in the typical whitewashed wooden clapboard, it would be fully covered in sandstone.

Centennial Memorial Hall was officially opened on October 9, 1884 (Figure 2.11), extolled with numerous speeches so long that a student today would shudder at the thought of attending such an occasion. The hall was named to commemorate the centenary of William Black initiating the first Canadian Methodist ministry which took place in Sackville. With two tall storeys above an elevated basement and a central tower, the 95-feet long by 52-feet wide structure was undertaken by the same architect/builder team who just fashioned the third male academy building across the street: Fairweather and Teed. Stylistically different than the third male academy building, Centennial Hall contained offices, classrooms, science labs in the basement, a generous library and a scientific museum on the second floor. It also housed the William Black Chapel with its exposed wooden roof ribs and a pair of large triple-lancet stained glass windows—one in memory of Black and the other for Charles Allison (Figure 2.12).

10. *The Chignecto Post* (December 28, 1882).

2.8 Dining room in the third male academy building

2.9 The third male academy building with the newly moved Commercial College building to the left, c.1917

2.10 The third male academy building connected to the Commercial College building and an additional storey added, c.1925

2.11 Centennial Memorial Hall (G. Ernest Fairweather, 1884)

2.12 William Black Chapel on the upper floor of Centennial Memorial Hall

The exterior was a fusion of Gothic Revival with some Second Empire thrown in via the addition of the mansard-roofed central tower. It was a time of eclecticism in architecture. The rules were flexible, especially when embedded in a time of wealth, and architecture is one of the best measures of a society's confidence in its present and its future. There is no denying that the 1880s were a time of grand civic and institutional swagger in New Brunswick, with the Second Empire as the figurehead style. Through the auspices of John A. Macdonald's National Policy, New Brunswick was enjoying an economically and culturally powerful upsurge in the new Canada, and this confidence is unmistakable in such Second Empire buildings as the Provincial Legislature (1882), the Saint John Custom House (1881) and Fredericton's City Hall (1876). The latter is noticeably similar to Centennial Hall—no coincidence as it was designed by the same architect (Figure 2.13).

With the Gothic expressed through the pointed windows and entry arch, stone trefoil finials at the gable peaks and rectangular windows with Gothic label molding, Centennial Hall had a foot in the spiritual door—which was welcome for the still-Methodist institution—while the verdant setting was equally valued by the romantics at the school in 1883:

The building is situated on one of the highest points of Sackville, with a healthful position, and from the tower one of the finest views in the Dominion can be commanded. The grounds, with proper care and a slight expense, can be made to add much to its beauty.[11]

Prosperity was growing, as was a real sense of ownership and stewardship for the institution. In 1886, Mount Allison was now officially recognized as a full-fledged university by the provincial government. That same year the school adopted cardinal and old gold as its official colours. An October 1889 issue of *The Wesleyan* hoped that "As the sons and daughters of Mount Allison acquire wealth, they will be sure to enrich their Alma Mater and lead her on to a magnificent future."[12] This anticipated philanthropy and support from alumni would indeed bear fruit in the coming generations.

The 1880s saw the ladies' academy and college go through somewhat of an identity crisis. Their founding mandate was to inspire and encourage high intellectual standards in the female students, but the era was increasingly making demands on

11. *The Argosy* (October 1883), p. 6. [MAA]

12. *The Wesleyan* (October 24, 1889).

2.13 Fredericton City Hall (McKean and Fairweather, 1876)

2.14 (L to R) Conservatory of Music building (G. Ernest Fairweather, 1891), the ladies' college building and Lingley Hall

young women to gain proper etiquette and social skills as well. It made sense that pursuits such as music and fine art could satisfy these goals while strengthening the women's programs at Mount Allison. Its 1883–84 catalogue read: "The tendency of the study of the Fine Arts to cultivate the taste and refine the manners, is fully recognized. Hence, adequate provision is made for a thorough and extended course of instruction in Vocal and Instrumental Music, and in Drawing and Painting."[13] Within a few years, the university would see a pair of new buildings dedicated to music and fine arts erected, and they would each be described as being among the best in the country.

The Mount Allison art school was applauded for its high quality of work, culminating in the introduction in 1887 of a four-year diploma program in Fine and Applied Arts—the first in Canada. As for music, the already respected program was greatly enriched by the arrival of professor Albert Mack from the United States, who, according to the Moncton *Daily Times* of June 1887, had "the expressed ambition … to make this department the *Conservatoire* of the Maritime provinces"[14] While the existing ladies' academy building had a passable suite of music rooms, in May 1888 the managers of the college pushed this ambition to the Alumnae Society and later the Board of Governors, encouraging them to raise money to build a dedicated conservatory of music for the ladies' college. They were convinced, and a campaign was launched the next month:

The loyalty and interest of old students in this work and the way they are taking hold of the enterprise, evidences their love for their Alma Mater. Collectors have been appointed in all the leading towns of the Maritime Provinces, and all the friends of Mount Allison earnestly requested to respond.[15]

Officially opened on June 2, 1891, the Conservatory of Music building was connected to the south wing of the ever-expanding ladies' college complex (Figure 2.14). Once again, G. Ernest Fairweather was the architect, and his stylistic output was becoming almost chameleon-like. This time he designed the building in the newly fashionable Queen Anne Revival style, complete with its characteristic irregular layout in plan, shape, colour and texture (Figure 2.15). The Queen Anne style is often considered Victorian architecture personified, with decorative opulence incorporating varied types of exterior shingles and siding, a somewhat

13. *Mount Allison Ladies' Academy Catalogue* (1883–84), p. 11. [MAA]

14. *Daily Times,* Moncton (June 2, 1887).

15. *The Argosy* (October 1888), p. 4. [MAA]

2.15 Conservatory of Music building, detail at main entry

medieval arrangement of steep hipped roofs, dormers, balconies, gables and chimneys, and the quintessential use of picturesque towers.

When compared to the earlier structures on the campus, the Conservatory of Music building was certainly audacious. Symmetry was starting to dissolve, as was architectural modesty. With its cone-roofed white towers shooting skyward like rockets, it stood guard over the town, commanding the crest of the hill like the iconic Neuschwanstein Castle in Bavaria. The elongated face of Mount Allison along the hill brow was now effectively a 'college row.' Found in a number of nineteenth-century American liberal arts colleges, such as those at Wesleyan University in Connecticut and Amherst College in Massachusetts, college rows are a tightly-knit arrangement of individual buildings of different styles and uses imparting almost a wall-like presence, and facing an open green space.

Mount Allison's new conservatory building contained 35 teaching and rehearsal rooms and a ground floor assembly room/gymnasium that could be used for large concerts and recitals. Known as Beethoven Hall, the room was tall and reasonably ornate with a raised stage at one end. Highlighted structural ribs at the walls and ceiling were richly adorned with milled trim and faux capitals below curved rib joints (Figure 2.16). The 1891 *Mount Allison Ladies' College Catalogue* inferred that the program and facilities were so good, they were unmatched anywhere in Canada. It was intended "to make it unnecessary for persons wishing to obtain a thorough and complete musical education, or to prepare themselves to teach music, to go outside of the Maritime Provinces."[16]

The last decade of the nineteenth century saw more program expansion at Mount Allison, with proposals for an engineering school and a "scientific cooking school in connection with the projected technological institute."[17] The establishment of these new subjects at the spiritually grounded Mount Allison were seen as extremely beneficial for offering engineers a broader arts-based outlook "under the very noblest moral influences"[18] as compared to other more secular schools. The man behind these proposals, science professor W.W. Andrews, felt that they would make the university "the leading educational institution of the province for the next 50 years."[19] In the ensuing years, Andrews introduced courses in biology and a more rigorous laboratory focus for the sciences of physics, chemistry and geology. Under such leadership, the upcoming 50th anniversary of the founding of the college was set to be filled with renewal and a bold "forward movement."[20]

16. *Mount Allison Ladies' College Catalogue* (1891), p. 43. [MAA]

17. John G. Reid, *Mount Allison University: A History* (Toronto: University of Toronto Press, 1984), vol. 1, p. 198.

18. *The Wesleyan* (May 28, 1891).

19. *The Wesleyan* (May 28, 1891).

20. *The Wesleyan* (April 23, 1891; May 7, 1891; May 21, 1891; May 28, 1891).

2.16 Beethoven Hall, Conservatory of Music building

This ebullience was echoed by the Saint John *Daily Sun* in 1894: "These are great days in the history of the Mt. Allison institutions. No previous period has seen so much activity and so many signs of growth and progress."[21] Growth and progress were burgeoning to be sure. The year was also one of celebration for the young men of the university as it saw the opening of the first dedicated residence for men in August of that same year (Figure 2.17). A partial result of having raised a semi-centennial memorial fund, the great stone building was erected in the large field on the opposite side of York Street from the campus. It was built by the now familiar contractor John Teed and designed by James C. Dumaresq, one of the greatest architects in the history of the Maritimes. It cost almost $70,000 and was intended to accommodate at least 100 students, with the option for future expansion. Boasting rich interior materials and state-of-the-art systems such as electric lights, forced hot air heating and running water, it was a far cry from the tired old mid-nineteenth-century College Hall that had become a student residence a decade before. Dumaresq's four-storey, 200-feet long residence was an assembly of load-bearing brick with stone trimmings, topped by a great mansard roof with a central tower. The main entry was flanked by turrets above, as well as two more turrets at the front corners of the main facade. Towards the back, a 90-feet long ell extended out, containing the kitchen and dining hall. This was a welcome change for the school as it was the first time the university students had their own dining hall, rather than having to share with the boys' academy.

The new residence stood tall and proud as a mammoth achievement in the town. The September 7, 1893, issue of *The Wesleyan* saw it as a sign of "large and generous faith in the future."[22] At the cornerstone-laying ceremony, President David Allison observed that if the contractors continued to perform as they had been, the boys would soon be "enjoying domiciliary comforts such as he when a lad rooming in the old Lodge had little dreamed."[23] Prompted by the opening of the new residence, *The Argosy* editorial of October 1894 set a lofty goal for Mount Allison, one that rings startlingly accurate right up to the present: "having been recognized for some years as the leading University of the Maritime Provinces, she now aspires to a higher dignity—a universal recognition as the leading University of Canada."[24]

Dumaresq looms large over the history of architecture in New Brunswick and Nova Scotia. He had a thriving career in Halifax during the 1870s, then, following opportunity, he moved to Saint John in 1877 to help rebuild the city after much

21. *The St. John Daily Sun* (June 1, 1894), p. 4.

22. *The Wesleyan* (September 7, 1893).

23. *The Argosy* (November 1893), p. 19. [MAA]

24. *The Argosy* (October 1894), p. 2. [MAA]

2.17 The first men's university residence (James C. Dumaresq, 1894)

of it had been destroyed by fire earlier that year. The highlight of his long career is the New Brunswick Legislature (1880–82), a monumental jewel of the Second Empire style. Although he moved back to Halifax in 1885, Dumaresq maintained a partnership with New Brunswick architect Harry Mott and continued to make a significant contribution to the architecture of the province. Sadly, Mount Allison's first men's residence building would be one of the university's, and Dumaresq's, most short-lived projects. It burned in June 1899. By the close of the nineteenth century, four of Mount Allison's major buildings had been lost to flames, and they would not be the last.

With the success of the Conservatory of Music building, attention turned to the other half of the ladies' college's cultural infrastructure. The art school's painting and drawing courses were an acknowledged success, but the addition of a well-appointed, designated art gallery in 1895 was instrumental in expanding the fine arts at Mount Allison. The gallery was incorporated into a new purpose-built building, and the basis of the art collection it housed was acquired from the former Owens Art Institution. Established in Saint John in 1884 as both an art school and a collection of European paintings, the Owens was experiencing financial difficulties. Faced with the threat of closure, the Owens moved to Mount Allison on the condition that an art gallery would be built to house the collection. It is difficult to say if those who lobbied to establish Mount Allison in Saint John in the early 1840s put up a fight to protect their financially troubled civic art institution, but the irony of Sackville acquiring the Owens should not be overlooked. With the Owens name and its collection of 400 paintings and about 100 plaster casts also came its director and primary instructor, John Hammond. Hammond is still renowned in the New Brunswick fine arts world for his international reputation, his achievement in developing one of Canada's best fine arts programs and for his impact on the architectural landscape of Sackville.

Once again, Mount Allison called on John Teed to erect the structure, with Edmund Burke of the Toronto firm Burke & Horwood as the architect. Burke was responsible for a prodigious number of important buildings in Toronto during the late nineteenth and early twentieth centuries, including the Simpsons department store, the Bloor Street Viaduct and the Royal Conservatory of Music. He was a pioneer in fusing American architectural advancements with European traditions, creating a uniquely Canadian form of expression. Caught in the race for height and light in the streets of downtown Toronto, Burke and his firm introduced the first curtain-wall construction to Canada.

Burke was the winner of a one-month design competition for the Owens, where six sets of plans were received from four architects. The jury chose Burke's rather Hellenistic submission that was an eclectic and robust interpretation of the symmetry and classical detailing of the Beaux-Arts style (Figure 2.18). Beaux Arts was the predominant architectural style of most civic and government buildings throughout North America and continental Europe between 1890 and 1920. Buildings in this style are characterized by grandiosity with an exuberance of detail inspired by Classical Roman and Greek temples, but set within layouts flaunting clear and ordered planning. The style's name derived from the École des Beaux-Arts in Paris, the most highly regarded architecture school in the world at that time, which emphatically encouraged this extravagant approach to design.

So how did Sackville attract the interest of one of Canada's most pre-eminent architects and the toast of Toronto to create such an architectural prize? The answer is simple enough: the love of a local woman. In 1881 Burke married Minnie Jane Black of Sackville. Her father was on the university's Board of Regents and he would have surely alerted Burke to the competition.

Burke's scheme for the Owens Art Gallery had three main gallery spaces behind an essentially windowless main facade of light olive sandstone on rusticated stone foundations. The smooth facades are decorated at the front with 'blind' colonnades holding up terracotta friezes. These lavish patterned friezes present organic patterns surrounding cherubs that hold up the names of artists such as Rembrandt, Turner and Raphael—inscribed clues to the giants of art history who inspired the glories that are contained within. The central entry door is surrounded by an *aedicule*—a Classical device encompassing the pair of Corinthian pilasters supporting a severe stone pediment, all surrounding an arched architectural recess. It's meant to evoke a shrine, giving note of the preciousness that is on the other side. Round ox-eye windows sit on either flank, giving it an almost face-like effect (Figure 2.19). This approach to the gallery, which was the main entry until the renovations of 1970–72 shifted it to the rear, would have been a key part of the processional character intended by Burke and the Beaux-Arts movement, where cultural monuments were seen as important civic focal points.

In exterior form, it is akin to a mini version of Charles McKim's landmark

2.18 Owens Art Gallery (Edmund Burke, 1895). This photograph was made near the end of the building's construction. Note that the terracotta friezes are not yet installed

2.19 Southern facade of the Owens Art Gallery centred on the original main entry

Boston Public Library of 1895. The overall plan of a central entry leading into a large gallery atrium space with two flanking galleries (Figure 2.20) would become common in comparable small art galleries, such as McKim, Mead and White's 1891 Walker Art Gallery at Bowdoin College in Maine, as well as the plan of the much later 1959 Beaverbrook Art Gallery in Fredericton.

In February 1894, *The Argosy* tantalized readers with this preview of what was to come for "the New Art Building":

The accepted plan for the new Art Building was that of Edmund Burke, of Toronto. This plan provides for a building 120 × 56, single storey, fronting on York Street. In front will be three connected exhibition rooms or galleries lighted by skylights. At the back there will be four work rooms, the first and largest for the drawing class, the second for the painting class, the third for the class in china painting, and the fourth for Professor Hammond's use. The galleries are very conveniently situated with regard to the workrooms, and are easy of access for students who are using as models the paintings and casts. Mr. Burke spent several days in Sackville examining the site and obtaining necessary data for maintaining his plan. Alternate tenders will be asked for from contractors, providing either for front and ends entirely of stone or for brick with stone facings.[25]

Officially opened on May 28, 1895, by Lieutenant-Governor John J. Fraser, the Owens Art Gallery and its art school accommodated three instructors and 45 students its first year, surrounded by the Owens' collection of pictures that all hung on the walls in what is now called a 'salon hanging'. This building, once called "without exception the finest art building in the Dominion of Canada",[26] is now the oldest university art gallery in the country. While its programs and courses were initially taken primarily by females, much later, following the Second World War, more men (many of them war veterans) entered the fine arts program, changing the dynamics and public perception of the department. Although the course instruction moved out of the building in 1965, the Owens Art Gallery still plays a vital role in the cultural life and vitality of the province. Mount Allison is fortunate to have such an extraordinary architectural work housing its great works of art.

Mention should be made of Edmund Burke's other Sackville projects, although they wouldn't officially become part of the Mount Allison landscape until long

25. *The Argosy* (February 1894), p. 17. [MAA]

26. *The Argosy* (January 1895), p. 7. [MAA]

2.20 Owens Art Gallery, interior view of central gallery atrium with the eastern flanking gallery and upper mezzanine visible, c.1900

2.21 John Hammond's residence, Hammond House, now the university president's residence (Edmund Burke, 1897)

after their completion. In the late 1890s, John Hammond engaged Burke to design a house and studio a block away from the campus on York Street. Set on large park-like grounds, it has become one of the most memorable homes in New Brunswick and a cherished part of the campus's built environment.

Hammond's 1897 residence is a sumptuous example of the Queen Anne style executed in the Maritime idiom of wood and shingles, with a lower level clad in local olive sandstone (Figure 2.21). Influenced by Classical elements as well as by the American Shingle Style of architecture, Hammond House sets a welcoming and varied tone, with the columned entry porch and round tower to the right offset by a lower gambrel-roofed wing to the left. Variety is paramount throughout the house, such as the odd sized gables at the roof, the oriel window at the upper floor, the arcaded side verandah and the assorted windows (bow, angled bay, Palladian, round-headed, oval) with decorative geometrical window mullions. Interior materials and details are rich, including beautiful stained wood finishes, a continuous mural frieze by Hammond in the dining room (Figure 2.22) and a great red sandstone fireplace designed by Sir William Van Horne. The house gained national attention when its plans and a large photograph of it were published in the November 1899 issue of *Canadian Architect and Builder*. In her book *Toronto Architect Edmund Burke*, Angela Carr considers that the interior plan, "unlike the open interior spaces and vast living halls of contemporary American designs, is compact—almost formal in its configuration—a concession, apparently, to the rigours of the Canadian climate."[27] Burke would design another three houses in Sackville over the next five years, some of which came in and out of Mount Allison's possession over time.

The John Hammond property was acquired by Mount Allison in 1958, and Hammond House became the official residence of the university president. After the university bought the nearby Cranewood for its 'new' president's house in 1975, Hammond House became administration and alumni offices. It was designated a National Historic Site of Canada in 1990, Sackville's first.

In 1903 Hammond renovated the adjacent barn (which pre-existed the house) into a summer painting studio, adding the series of six giant red-sandstone pillars (Figure 2.23). The robust supports helped frame and heighten the presence of what the *Allisonia* predicted could be "one of the finest studios in Canada."[28] These pillars are some of the largest pieces ever quarried by the Sackville Freestone

27. Angela Carr, *Toronto Architect Edmund Burke* (Montreal: McGill-Queens University Press, 1995), p. 70.

28. *Allisonia* (November 1903), p. 17. [MAA]

2.22 Hammond House, mural frieze by John Hammond in dining room

2.23 John Hammond's barn and summer studio (1903), later Bermuda House residence

Company, whose pit only 100 yards away would eventually supply the red sandstone for most of Mount Allison's buildings (Figure 2.24). While this stone was also used on Centennial Hall years before, the real story begins in 1898 when Charles Pickard opened a permanent quarry to harvest the enormous outcrop of sandstone on his farm. Buildings throughout the Maritimes and Ontario used the quarry's fine stone, which was described by *The Canadian Architect and Builder* magazine as extending "over 15 to 20 acres of Mr. Pickard's farm, at a depth of 3 to 15 feet from the surface" with "unlimited quantities" being available. The material was a rich shade of reddish-brown, and was "pronounced first-class in quality."[29] Mount Allison purchased the quarry in 1930, becoming one of very few universities in North America to own its own building stone quarry. Now filled almost completely with water, the open quarry has been dormant for decades.

Around 1909, the next owner of Hammond House, Fred Ryan, added a barn/carriage house beside the studio. The barn was turned into apartments in 1947, but in 1984–85 it and the Hammond Studio were joined by an all-weather corridor and renovated into a student residence known as Bermuda House.

Hammond himself became an accomplished designer of houses (two of his 1900s houses still stand near the campus) and of landscape features such as the campus gates at the end of Lansdowne Street and the swan pond fountain. One of the most picturesque and familiar features on the campus, the swan pond (Figure 2.25) is actually an artificial lake that came to be after the Charles Allison house (on the site of Convocation Hall) burned in 1898 and the ladies' college principal, Byron Borden, saw an opportunity to alter the surrounding landscape. The pond was excavated in 1901 according to drawings by John Hammond, who specified two islands in the design. By November, underground waterlines were in place to supply the water, and by December, students were skating on the frozen white ice (Figure 2.26).

A.D. Morton, a Mount Allison alumnus of 1864, couldn't hold back his awe after visiting the campus in 1899; imagining the persistent architectural evolution that continued to build on the foundations of the old: "The first half century in the history of these Institutions has witnessed great progress, but they are only as yet in their initial stages of development. Fifty years from now! But my mind staggers. My pen is inadequate to the portrayal of what will be."[30]

29. *The Canadian Architect and Builder* (February 1900), p. 44.

30. *The Wesleyan* (December 27, 1899).

2.24 Sackville Freestone Company quarry, early twentieth century

2.25 Mount Allison's swan pond, with the Conservatory of Music building, the ladies' college building, and Hart Hall in the background

2.26 Students skating on the frozen swan pond, c.1902

CHAPTER THREE

Noble Responses to the New Century

1900–1945

Prime Minister Wilfrid Laurier asserted in 1904 that "Canada has been modest in its history, although its history, in my estimation, is only commencing. It is commencing in this century. The nineteenth century was the century of the United States. I think we can claim that Canada will fill the twentieth century."[1] So too would this small campus on the marsh that came of age in the nineteenth century, under the shadow of larger and more central colleges and universities, assert itself on the national and international stage in the twentieth century. Mount Allison's history had also only commenced, and its great maturing would hit its stride in the new century, punctuated by new architecture and loftier campus plans.

The twentieth century rolled out with Mount Allison reeling from more fire devastation. The first men's residence building burned to the ground after only five years of service on June 11, 1899, and Burke and Horwood's architectural talents were called upon again to design the second men's university residence building, which opened in September 1900 (Figures 3.1, 3.2).

Although the $70,000 first residence building was only insured for $45,000, the Board of Regents met nine days after the fire and felt "there should be no retrogression in any respect,"[2] boldly pushing that a new residence be built on the same charred site. In retrospect, the fire could have been much worse. It was reported that the nearby Owens Art Gallery was saved by John Hammond and several others who had the courage to continuously pour water on the roof to extinguish flying sparks.

The new residence would have opened a full semester earlier, had it not been for a serious wind and rain storm which blew down the partially completed stone walls in October 1899. Natural and human disasters notwithstanding, when the

1. Wilfrid Laurier, in a speech to the Canadian Club, Ottawa, January 18, 1904.

2. *Minutes of the Board of Regents* (1899–1920), pp. 1–2. [MAA]

3.1 The second men's university residence (Burke and Horwood, 1900)

3.2 Students in front of the second men's university residence, 1912

building was finally completed the university calendar claimed it "combines conditions exceptionally conducive to health and agreeable living, and may challenge comparison with any students' residence in Canada."[3] Although there were some student complaints regarding the residence's exterior aesthetics and poor ventilation, great pride was taken in the food service (Figure 3.3), even in those early days of dietary science:

3. *Mount Allison Calendar* (1900), pp. 38–41. [MAA]

4. *Hand book of the Institutions of Mount Allison: The Central Institutions of the Maritime Provinces* (Sackville: Eurhetorian Society of Mount Allison University, 1903), p. 49. [MAA]

5. *The Canadian Architect and Builder* (December 1900), p. 233.

The food supplied in the dining room is excellent. It is always well cooked and daintily prepared, as great a variety as possible being aimed at. In the autumn when a number of men are training, several tables are set apart as training tables and here the athletes have a style of food given to them conducive to muscle building.[4]

Closely matching its predecessor in size at 217 feet by 50 feet with a 90 feet by 45 feet ell, the Romanesque Revival stone and brick behemoth appeared taller due to its low hip roof and central tower with its arrow-like peak. While it was forced to match its predecessor's floor-plate boundaries, the eclectic treatment of its volume and asymmetrical towers were entirely Burke's. Undeniably impressive, the residence was still somewhat disjointed compared with his other work, lacking the conceptual unity and geometrical rigour he was recognized for. But even with this, the structure was strongly praised in the press. According to the December 1900 issue of *The Canadian Architect and Builder*:

The students' rooms are bright, airy and commodious, and present alternating systems of rooms in pairs (study and bedroom for two), with apartments for single occupancy. The large hall in the ell is a handsome room having an open truss roof with exposed timbers, and ornamented windows.

The building contains [a] spacious and sunny dining room, well lighted reading rooms, large office and reception rooms, Y.M.C.A. rooms and rooms set apart for hospital uses.[5]

To guard against the Mount Allison fire curse, the residence had red slate roofs, brick interior firewalls, a sophisticated system of water-hoses throughout, and a large reservoir in one of the towers. While the seemingly thorough fire prevention systems would prove ineffective several decades later, the ventilation complaint

3.3 Dining hall in the second men's university residence building

(and the students' subsequent response for getting fresh air) would paradoxically end up saving lives when a fire did occur in 1941.

As programs continued to expand at Mount Allison, a new applied science department was created, with the understanding that it would allow advanced admission to engineering programs such as that at McGill University. In 1903 the cold and tired Old Lodge building was lifted and renovated into the McClelan School of Applied Science (Figure 3.4), named after its fundraising champion A.R. McClelan, a Mount Allison Academy student in the 1840s who later became Lieutenant-Governor of New Brunswick. So the university now had proper facilities for the study of physics, chemistry, biology, geology and engineering, all of which used to be taught in crowded facilities in the basement of Centennial Hall. From what *The Argosy* called "the most spacious scientific building in this part of Canada,"[6] students were now able to complete the first two years in architecture and civil, electrical, mining and mechanical engineering in preparation for completion at McGill and several other technical universities. This specialized focus was seen as a critical contribution to the industrial and economic health of the Maritimes, and the McClelan building would be crucial to the school's new technical mission. The aforementioned Maritimes goal dovetailed nicely with the University of New Brunswick's new science/engineering building that opened at the Fredericton campus two years earlier in 1901, proving that New Brunswick was taking applied science seriously. The McClelan building was renovated and expanded in the early 1920s, but like so many of its relatives, it would ultimately burn to the ground a decade later.

Beyond these academic additions, more living quarters were needed for the steadily growing student body. The first decade of the twentieth century would see the total enrollment of all three Mount Allison institutions rise by 80 percent between 1900–01 and 1910–11. Connected to the rear of the ladies' college building, a brick annex named Borden Hall opened in January 1904 (Figure 3.5), containing a kitchen, a large dining hall with Venetian tracery windows, a hospital (Figure 3.7) and rooms to accommodate 40 more students. Borden Hall was designed by Edmund Burke and built by contractor James Reid of Sydney, Nova Scotia. It was called "a magnificent four storied, brick building … fitted throughout with the most modern conveniences."[7] Progress was contagious as in 1910 the male academy building across the road saw its upper floor converted from

67

6. *The Argosy* (November 1903), p. 47. [MAA]

7. *The Argosy* (November 1903), p. 48. [MAA]

3.4 McClelan School of Applied Science building, c.1921–33

3.5 Borden Hall (Edmund Burke, 1904) is the brick wing in the centre of the photograph. The former female academy gymnasium (clapboard building on right) was renovated to house the Lillian Massey-Treble School of Household Science in 1903–04

"an unfinished attic inhabited by bats and the appurtenances of ancient water systems"[8] to rooms for 36 new students. Electric lights were installed throughout the entire building. The magic of electricity was likewise fitted around the same time throughout the ladies' college building. It is amusing to compare a circa 1891 photo of their reception room with its oil lamp chandelier (Figure 3.6) with a typical female residence room circa 1914, the subjects obviously less than enthused about the technology above their heads (Figure 3.8).

With the new ladies' dining hall in place, the former dining hall (the old ladies' college gymnasium) was refitted as the Lillian Massey-Treble School of Household Science (Figure 3.5). While it may not seem quite as reformist today, the School of Household Science was seen as a female equivalent to the male-centric School of Applied Science. Courses in "domestic science" or "domestic chemistry" would be offered as training for future teachers, with emphasis on the study of food products and home hygiene. Typical of the gender biases of the era, in May 1904 *The Sackville Tribune* projected that the new facility would ensure that "girls will go out from this school fully equipped to grapple with domestic difficulties and as veritable household angels, to comfort and bless."[9] This curriculum, subsequently modified, lasted well into modern times. As John Reid noted, "Along with Music and the Fine Arts, household science—or 'home economics' as it was later known—would be one of the three ladies' college departments to survive the demise of that institution. It would continue to be taught at the university until suspended in 1971."[10]

With all this growth, the problem of crowding and obsolete buildings needed to be addressed. The mid nineteenth-century Lingley Hall auditorium needed replacing, and a powerful local family saw an opportunity to erect a working memorial to its patriarch. One of Sackville's largest employers, the Fawcett Foundry was established in 1852, producing stoves and cast metal items at its large production and warehouse facility near the northern edge of the Mount Allison campus. In 1908 *The Sackville Tribune* proclaimed the foundry to be "one of Eastern Canada's leading industrial concerns" with showrooms "superior to the show-rooms of any other stove manufacturers in the whole Dominion."[11] The Fawcett family was in a position to spend at will, and spend it did on a structure that even the ancient Romans would have recognized as familiar and important.

Extending below the hilltop limits of the campus, Charles Fawcett Memorial

8. *The Mount Allison Year Book* (1931), p. 116. [MAA]

9. *The Sackville Tribune* (May 19, 1904), p. 7.

10. John G. Reid, *Mount Allison University: A History* (Toronto: University of Toronto Press, 1984), vol. 1, p. 241.

11. *The Sackville Tribune* (December 21, 1908), p. 8.

3.6 Ladies' college building, reception room, c.1891

3.7 The ladies' college hospital, located in Borden Hall

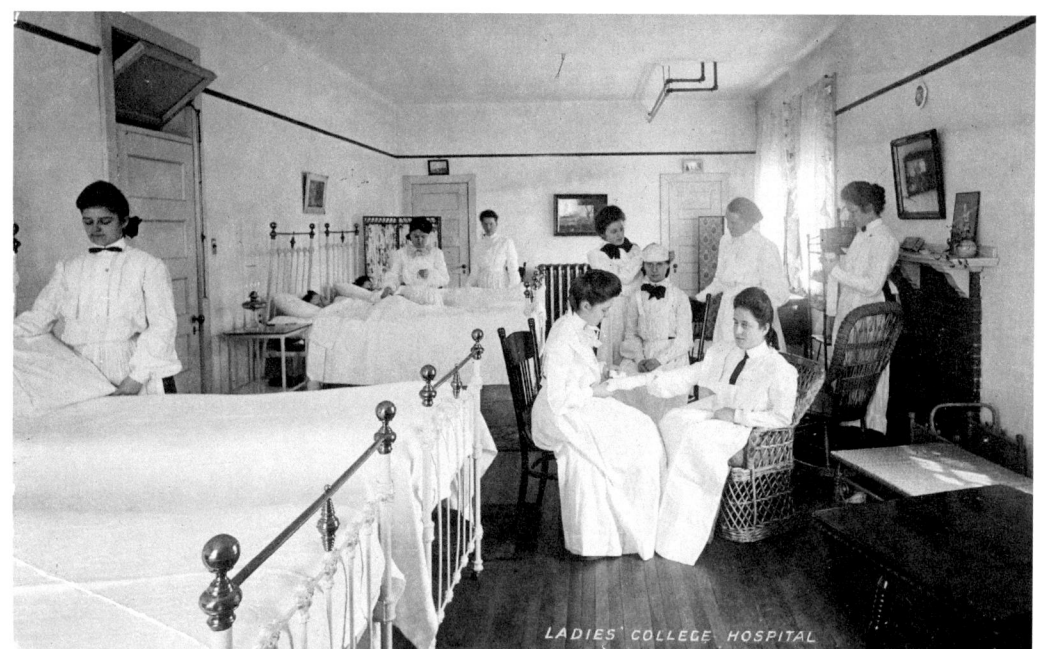

3.8 A typical ladies' college residence room, c.1914

Hall was built facing York Street with the swan pond behind. Lingley Hall's architectural cues were compelling, and Fawcett Hall was deeply inspired by its Classical language (Figure 3.10). While not an exact copy, the design of Fawcett Hall was similar enough to that of Lingley Hall that Lingley's designers might be considered co-designers of the new auditorium building. At its official opening on May 26, 1910, the 125-feet long by 84-feet wide Fawcett Hall stood proudly behind its white Ionic columns. They held up a pediment decorated with three huge female figures representing the Muses of Greek mythology: Calliope (the middle figure) holding a scroll embodies poetry and writing; Euterpe, with a lyre, symbolizes music; and Terpsichore, outfitted with a drum, embodies dance. The carvings (now sadly lost) were ideal sculptural symbols for an avowedly Classical building designed for performance, at a school with a deep-seeded alliance with, and esteem for, women.

Harmonizing with the growing university, Fawcett Hall's lofty auditorium hall could accommodate 1200 people (Figure 3.9), while the stage could hold 300 more—about double the capacity of Lingley Hall. The *Saint John Globe* said that once it becomes fully decorated and the paintings hung on the inside, "the institution will have one of the finest auditoriums in the Dominion."[12] At its official opening, Fawcett Hall was praised as a symbol of the mutual contributions of business and education, and it saw four very successful concerts take place in three days.

The architect of Fawcett Hall was Willard M. Mitchell and the contractor was Victor Woodworking, both of nearby Amherst, Nova Scotia. Known as much as an artist of miniatures as he was a designer of buildings, Mitchell was born in Saint John and apprenticed with leading Saint John architects R.C. John Dunn and John McKean. In 1904 he taught painting at the Mount Allison Ladies' College for a year, which would have introduced him to the university's administrators. By early 1907 he had relocated to Amherst, where he was active as an architect until he moved to Ontario in 1923 and became a full-time painter.

Fawcett Hall was a handsome building, fitting for both its purpose and site. The interior was finished with cypress wood, stained a rich brown. Overflowing with historical meaning, this use of cypress prompted the May 1910 *Allisonia* to predict that since "pieces of cypress many thousands of years old may be seen in museums we are inclined to think that Fawcett Hall will be an everlasting monument."[13] Regrettably, this Sackville cypress was not as persuasive. For 55 consecutive years

12. *Saint John Globe* (February 7, 1910), p. 2.

13. *Allisonia* (May 1910), p. 104. [MAA]

3.9 Charles Fawcett Memorial Hall, interior view

3.10 Charles Fawcett Memorial Hall (Willard M. Mitchell, 1910)

convocation services were held here, as were Founder's Day ceremonies, concerts, plays, speeches and assemblies. In so many ways Fawcett Hall was the public face of Mount Allison University until it was demolished in June 1965 to make way for the present Convocation Hall.

With the hubbub focused on the new facilities, what would become of the now vacant Lingley Hall? Up until then, Mount Allison rarely had the chance to consider options for older, vacated buildings as they usually burned to a charred mess before such considerations needed to be made. In the case of Lingley Hall, thought had been given to carefully tearing it down and salvaging its materials for the imminent Fawcett Hall. What eventually happened in 1910 was that it was moved from its original site adjacent to the ladies' college building to a location down the hill near the swan pond. There, the poised old edifice stood for several years, decaying like an ancient ruin in the Roman Forum—abandoned, but still surrounded by active, occupied buildings. Because it had hosted the university's graduations and main ceremonies for 55 years (coincidentally, the same as Fawcett), alumni disdain for its state was palpable, and something had to be done. Principal James M. Palmer later remembered the situation as "the greatest snarl and biggest or knottiest question for solution I ever knew at Mt. A."[14] Halifax poet and alumnus Matthew Ritchey Knight wrote these lines aching for Lingley Hall in the May 1910 *Allisonia*:

> *Daughters mine, behold my shame,*
> *Torn from mine ancient place.*
> *Sharers are ye in all my fame,*
> *Sharers in my disgrace.*
> *Torn from the spot where I once stood*
> *Since I am old and gray,*
> *And fit not with the finer mood*
> *And fashion of to-day.*
> *Another occupies my throne,*
> *And lords it from the hill;*
> *But winged hosts of memories grown*
> *Thro' long years haunt it still.*[15]

14. Letter from Palmer to W.T.R. Flemington, October 31, 1932. [MAA, Flemington Papers, 7835–8]

15. *Allisonia* (May 1910), p. 111. [MAA]

3.11 Gymnasium, formerly Lingley Hall (renovated, 1912)

16. *The Argosy* (February 1921), p. 195. [MAA]

17. *Allisonia* (March 1910), pp. 76–77. [MAA]

By early 1912, Lingley Hall was disassembled and rebuilt near the men's residence building and football field, finding an unexpected new role as the university's gymnasium (Figure 3.11). This function was short-lived, as the building was destroyed by fire in 1921. So too was a captured First World War German Fokker aircraft that was hanging from the upper ceiling beams. *The Argosy* reported that "In an incredibly short time the flames had mounted to such a height that it was impossible for the student-fire-fighters to reach the blaze with their buckets, and they then turned their attention to salvaging as much of the athletic apparatus as possible."[16] Anyone as yet unconvinced that fire is at the heart of Mount Allison's architectural chronicle should consider that the first dedicated men's college gymnasium opened in 1877 only to be destroyed by fire in January 1883; it was replaced with a second men's college gymnasium in 1887, which burned to the ground in 1912. Hence the need to convert the somewhat extravagant Lingley Hall into the new gym.

Freeing up the former Lingley Hall site enabled Mount Allison to engage Edmund Burke one last time. Burke designed Jairus Hart Hall, a new four-storey north wing attached to the ladies' college building (Figure 3.12). Originally containing women's residence rooms, classrooms, a gym and an apartment for the college principal, this 1910 building was consciously different from its connected partner in that it was built not of wood, but of stone (Figure 3.13). Both its dignified sturdiness and local availability made the material a perfect choice for the building's shell, as well as the perceived fireproofness of the material. Tendered at just over $44,000, the rock-faced red and olive sandstone structure with its hip roof, varied dormers and angled bays was admired immediately upon its completion, almost to the detriment of the ladies' college building:

Hart Hall has at last, after much eager anticipation on the part of its would-be occupants, opened its doors for occupation. All expectations are more than realized and it is indeed a pleasure to visit the beautiful rooms with their snowy walls, smooth hard-wood floors and fresh new furniture. The corridors are wide and bright and altogether the new wing is good to look upon. With a few more wings, such as that we could almost dispense with the body.[17]

3.12 View of Mount Allison buildings atop the college hill, c.1910. At the far right, connected to the ladies' college building, is Jairus Hart Hall (Burke & Horwood, 1910)

3.13 Jairus Hart Hall, detail of exterior stone

3.14 Jairus Hart Hall, annex wing, 1920

18. *The Argosy* (November 1914), p. 116–117. [MAA]

Repeatedly modified, Hart Hall would have a 'New Hall' annex link built on in 1920 (Figure 3.14) which boasted a small 12 feet by 32 feet swimming pool at the lower level (Figure 3.15). The entire building would later house such facilities as a hospital, the university bookstore, fine arts studios and an electrical shop, in addition to classrooms and offices. Generations of soot and grime have darkened the skin of the building, making the red and olive blocks seem mostly a uniform dark brown, but underneath is an attractive masonry pattern that visually punches the multiple window shapes and outside corners.

When B.C. Borden, the former principal of the Mount Allison Ladies' College, was installed as the university's president in 1911, he started pushing for reform at Mount Allison. Financial strains were ever-present, and the university was becoming more rigourous in its degree programs. A full bachelor of music program was created, one of the few offered in Canada, and the new BSc program produced its first graduate in 1918. The present day academic framework of Mount Allison was beginning to form.

At the close of the nineteenth century, the sporting culture we now take for granted at universities was also taking shape. Organized rugby teams started to appear at Mount Allison in 1890, a hockey team was started in 1896, while cricket was played several decades before. Women's sports were in the mix as well, with basketball and hockey teams formed in the 1901–02 academic year.

Then everything changed. The world would soon witness the death of millions through a hellish imperial war, and Mount Allison would pay a heavy price. While the declaration of war in August 1914 didn't immediately affect the university or academy, the rumblings of the First World War would change much at the school. Virtually all of the male students enrolled for military training on campus through an officers' training corps. *The Argosy* was hauntingly accurate in its assessment of what was to come:

The impression is gaining ground that the struggle now being waged in Europe is likely to be long and tedious. Many students who would like to respond to the call of the Empire wish to finish the college year upon which they have entered. A course of systematic training during the winter months would make such men valuable additions to a regiment in the spring.[18]

3.15 Jairus Hart Hall, swimming pool, 1920

The rush was on as it was announced in December 1914 that the Lingley Hall gymnasium would be refitted as a drill hall, with "work to be commenced at once."[19] Such changes did constrain the lives of some. The female students were suddenly not allowed to visit nearby Amherst without a chaperone, due to the great influx of soldiers and the risks assumed about such a testosterone-laden environment. Enrollment would soon drop dramatically, and it was claimed that a larger proportion of Mount Allison students enlisted in the services than in any other college or university in Canada. But such inconveniences paled in comparison to the mounting losses that would start to hit home by 1915. As John Reid recounted in his history of Mount Allison:

The Argosy of October 1915—the opening issue of the 1915–16 year—carried the first in what was to be a long series of obituaries of Allisonians who had died at the front. Gordon V. Boone, a graduate of 1911, had been killed by shrapnel in April; Vernon C. Elderkin of the class of 1912 had been killed by a shell explosion in May; Arthur Mackay had died of spinal meningitis 'somewhere in France.' ... By the time the war ended, 73 from Mount Allison had died.[20]

The jovial spirit and lively student life of the university was dissolving, burdened with circumstances *The Argosy* sadly observed: "The Residence, once crammed to its doors, sends back a hollow echo from rooms whose former occupants are 'somewhere in France,' and the occasional hilarity of midnight gatherings is saddened by the thoughts of those who might have been here."[21] The strain on the university was not only social and emotional, but financial as well. Registration and tuition income were down to crisis levels, and a late-1916 fundraising appeal was supported in *The Wesleyan* magazine, which pleaded with Maritime Methodists to not "let Mount Allison be crippled through the patriotism of her sons."[22] Burdens were so heavy that serious consideration was given to close the university for the duration of the war. The armistice of late 1918 couldn't have come soon enough.

Following the end of the First World War, change was in the air, especially when it came to the relationship of the sexes. Previously, female residents of Mount Allison had to sign out every time they left the residence, even for classes. Dances and co-ed socials were not allowed, and female and male students could only

19. *The Sackville Tribune* (December 14, 1914).

20. John G. Reid, *Mount Allison University: A History* (Toronto: University of Toronto Press, 1984), vol. 2, p. 8.

21. *The Argosy* (October 1915), pp. 56–57. [MAA]

22. *The Wesleyan* (December 6, 1916).

see one another during church. In fact, college women were required to travel to and from church in two straight, quiet lines. Whether it was in recognition of the contribution of women during the war or simply the relaxing of social mores, after 1918 there was a noticeable easing of such restrictions, both at Mount Allison and at other Canadian universities.

Spartan by today's standards, Mount Allison's two athletic buildings built immediately after the First World War—College Rink (1920, Figure 3.16) and the 'temporary' gymnasium (1921, Figure 3.17)—would have been considered miles ahead of the facilities they replaced. The rink was a typical Canadian indoor arena of the era, with huge wooden trusses spanning above the ice surface and bare bench seating behind jagged boards. Built on Lansdowne Street opposite the current Athletic Centre, it would be replaced by Allison Gardens in 1948. A misnomer if there ever was one on the campus, the temporary gym building would be used for the next four decades until the Athletic Centre opened in 1961. Briefly used as a student centre in the 1960s, the stained Douglas-fir-lined gym was demolished in 1968 to make way for student residences. The temporary gym's architect was a young Charles A. Fowler of Halifax, a Mount Allison alumnus who would soon expand his reach by contributing several major designs to the Mount Allison scene, as well as many notable churches, schools and hospitals throughout the Maritimes.

Buildings were starting to fall into two distinct categories at Mount Allison: those which were purely functional and economical with little or no aesthetic intention (i.e., the rink and gym), and those which conveyed their worth and function through rich materials and formal design. Belying the short lifespan of many of the university's structures up to this time (often due to fire) was the desire for buildings that conveyed a deep sense of permanence. Around the turn of the century, North American universities were striving to look affectedly 'old', if not timeless. They believed their campuses had to exude tradition, giving donors a sense that their bricks and mortar gifts radiated style and endurance.

Enter the Collegiate Gothic style. Although the mid-nineteenth-century North American Gothic Revival is closely tied to New Brunswick through the abundance of nineteenth-century Carpenter Gothic houses and Bishop John Medley's Anglican churches (such as the 1857 St. Paul's facing Mount Allison from Main Street), a later Gothic Revival that spanned the 1900s to the 1930s is equally remarkable. Collegiate Gothic is the evocative name given to the late Gothic Revival employed

3.16 Mount Allison's College Rink, 1920

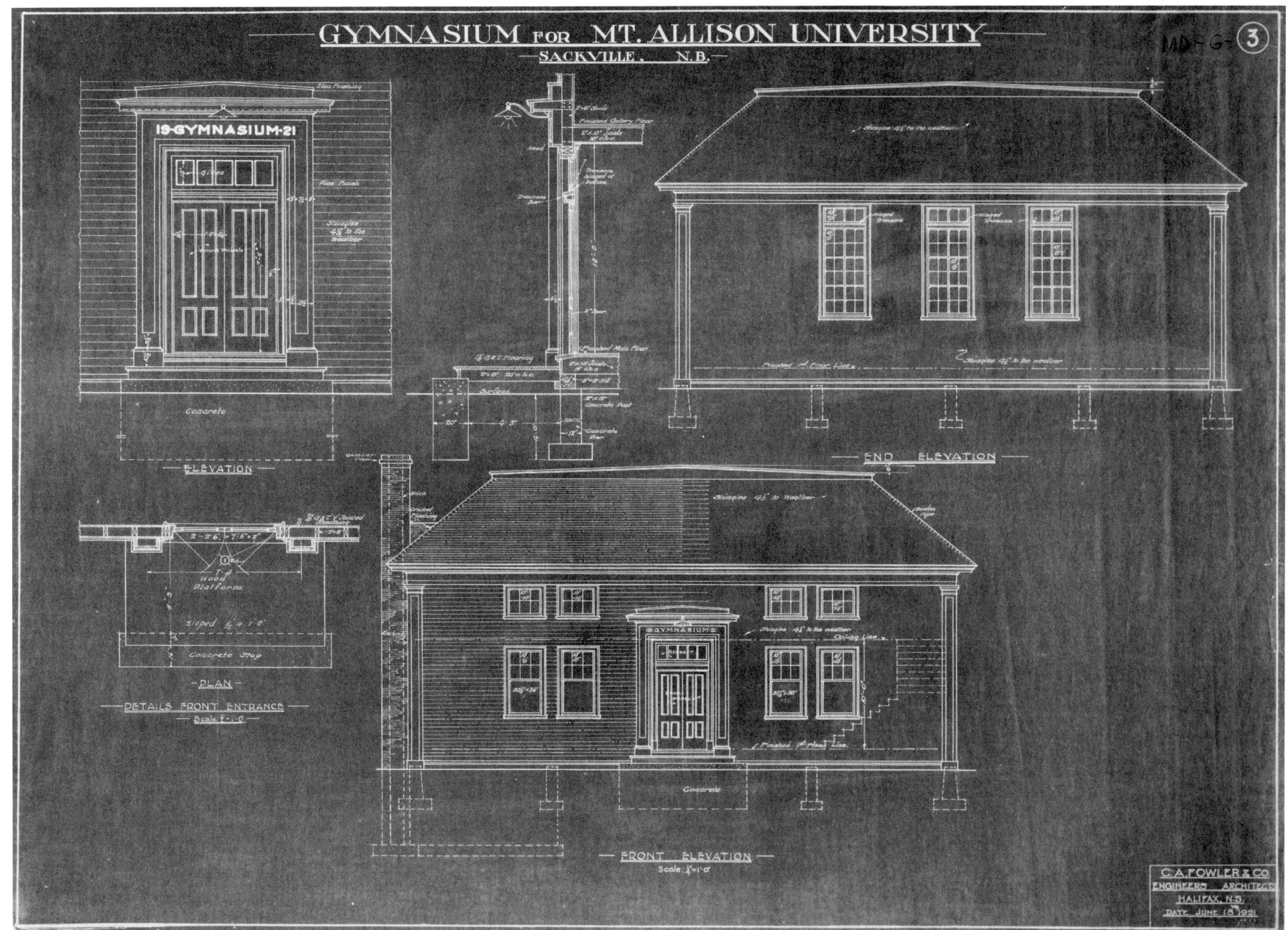

3.17 Architectural drawing of Mount Allison's 'temporary' gymnasium (C.A. Fowler & Co., 1921)

23. W. Bruce Leslie, "Dreaming Spires in New Jersey: Anglophilia in Wilson's Princeton," in *The Educational Legacy of Woodrow Wilson: From College to Nation*, ed. James Axtell (Charlottesville: University of Virginia Press, 2012), p. 102.

at countless university campuses throughout North America during the early twentieth century. Affectionately based on the period style and approach of medieval British universities such as Oxford and Cambridge, the Collegiate Gothic dominated campus architecture in the United States and Canada for decades. Post-1910 reconstruction gave a renewed Gothic face to such institutions as Yale, Boston College, Princeton, the University of Toronto, McGill and the University of Saskatchewan. In 1902, future American President Woodrow Wilson, then president of Princeton and apparently a closet architect himself, was a strong advocate for the style: "By the very simple device of building our new buildings in the Tudor Gothic style we seem to have added to Princeton the age of Oxford and Cambridge; we have added a thousand years to the history of Princeton by merely putting those lines in our buildings which point every man's imagination to the historic traditions of learning in the English-speaking race."[23] While this reads today as very Anglocentric, one does get the picture of how those in power saw the importance of architectural character. The style made fewer inroads in New Brunswick compared to the rest of Canada, but Mount Allison was enriched with a handful of notable Collegiate Gothic buildings with their prominent arched entries, antique window patterns, substantial stone masonry and carved ornament.

As its name suggests, the Memorial Library was built to honour the 73 Mount Allison students and alumni who were killed in the First World War. The tangible working memorial was the work of Halifax's pre-eminent architect of the early twentieth century, Andrew R. Cobb, who would later design the new science building and help rebuild Centennial Hall. Cobb was one of the first academically trained architects in the Maritimes. Rather than undertaking a traditional apprenticeship, Cobb attended the Massachusetts Institute of Technology (graduating in 1903), followed by further studies at the École des Beaux-Arts in Paris. In 1909 he set up shop in Halifax and went on to eventually design some of the principal buildings at Dalhousie and Acadia Universities, making him one of the most experienced collegiate architects in the Maritimes.

The specific choice of a library being the war memorial was entirely appropriate. After the smoke cleared from the war and the scale of the carnage was understood, there was little choice but to erect a building of influence and inspiration that would be used by everyone. The university regents wasted no time, as a motion was passed on November 26, 1918—just two weeks after the armistice—to pursue a library and start fundraising. The details and aspirations of the memorial campaign were cited in the February 1919 *Mount Allison Record*:

This Memorial Library will be most unique both in its significance and in its utilitarianism. It will be nothing short of a capitalization of the sacrificial bravery of the students of the Past for the practical use and inspiration of the generations of the future. It will moreover, fulfill a crying need of the Institutions. There are those who argue so would a Science Building, a University Women's Residence, a Central Heating Plant. But just here we face a difficulty. Though these too, are urgent needs, yet they are not the needs of the three institutions as a whole, as is the call for a Library, and in none of these could we so well symbolize the sacrifices made. For after all there is something sacred about a Library and here more than on any other spot on the campus, hovers that mysterious but very real something, the College Spirit.[24]

Exuding dignity and craftsmanship, the library opened to the enthusiastic student body in June 1927 (Figure 3.19). The $100,000 building was a bold and sturdy statement: a three-storey red Sackville sandstone mass under a large steeply-pitched gable roof covered in dark grey slate. Prominently Tudor Gothic in style, which was called by the *Mount Allison Record* "the most suitable for college buildings,"[25] its carved window trim and coping stones were olive Dorchester sandstone. Although it was a secular building, the sacred was still front and centre as its main approach imparted a chapel essence with its simple rectangular form, along with the continuous string of tall windows at the upper floor. The building's main entry was through a Tudor-arched double door in a fortress-like porch guarded by a crenellated roof (suitably evoking both the Gothic age and the military). The rear of the library had a more varied appearance, with a large bay window around the main stair atop a deep ell wing.

The substantial bay window and main staircase were arresting when entering the building, striking the viewer head-on with its glazed grid of light (Figure 3.18). The beautiful staircase split into three at a wide windowed landing, leading to the great reading room (Figure 3.20). The pièce de résistance of the interior, the reading room, was a vast 80 feet by 36 feet open space under a vaulted ceiling, with a circulation desk to the side and book stack space behind—the way that library books were sometimes accessed up until mid century. The rest of the areas were

24. *Mount Allison Record*, February 1919, pp. 1–2. [MAA]

25. *Mount Allison Record*, November, 1926, p. 65. [MAA]

3.18 Memorial Library, interior staircase

3.19 Memorial Library (Andrew R. Cobb, 1927)

3.20 Memorial Library, reading room

taken up by library-related offices, washrooms, an archives, study rooms, university administration offices and a large 'memorial hall' at the centre of the main floor which contained the memorial tablets emblazoned with 73 names.

The confidence of the 1920s was starting to drive overwhelming growth at the university. While it took 30 years for the student body to double from 141 to 278 between 1894 and 1925, in only a few years it mushroomed to 400 students by 1928. The resulting crunch for space even forced the university to temporarily lease two of Sackville's largest hotels and convert them into a women's residence they called Allison Lodge, and a men's residence branded simply 'The Lodge'. A million-dollar campaign was launched in early 1929 aimed at the building of a science building and women's residence for the university, and a school and laboratory building for the male academy, as well as adding $400,000 to the endowment fund. Cobb was engaged to design the three buildings, which were noticeably Classical in their appearance (Figure 3.21). Ink renderings published in a campaign booklet entitled *Mount Allison is Yours* look very similar to Cobb's designs at Dalhousie University, not to mention deviating with the Gothicism of his recent Memorial Library building, which may have led to their revisiting for stylistic reasons. It is also interesting to note where these three were proposed to sit. None were even close to where their eventual versions would be sited (Figure 3.22).

Cobb's Neoclassical plans never saw the light of day. The onslaught of the stock market crash drew the schools' expansion plans to a screeching halt. A year after the campaign launch, less than half of the projected funds had been raised. As the Great Depression deepened in the 1930s, only one of three proposed buildings was constructed; the sizeable bequest that was to finance it was completely wiped out by the crash. So as buildings were going up, so too was the university's debt.

In the midst of the Great Depression, a large new science building was planned to replace the stretched-to-its-limit McClelan building. *Mount Allison is Yours* held nothing back with regards to the present building's deficiencies:

Experience has proved that no University class should exceed 30 students; yet Mt. Allison is forced to put 95 and even more into some of hers, because of lack of space and equipment. The Chemistry Department, now housed in the oldest building

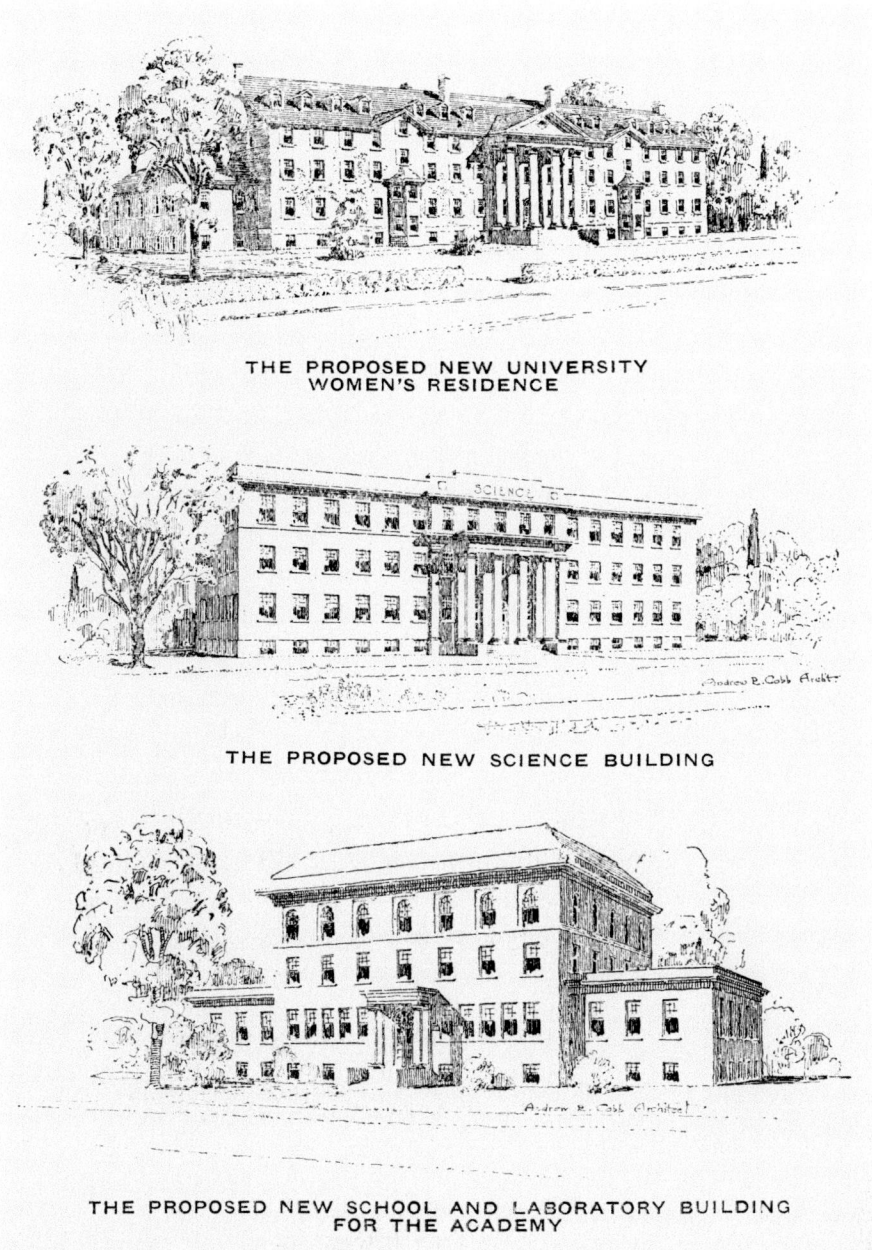

THE PROPOSED NEW UNIVERSITY
WOMEN'S RESIDENCE

THE PROPOSED NEW SCIENCE BUILDING

THE PROPOSED NEW SCHOOL AND LABORATORY BUILDING
FOR THE ACADEMY

3.21 Proposed designs for a new Mount Allison women's residence building, science building and male academy building (Andrew R. Cobb, 1928)

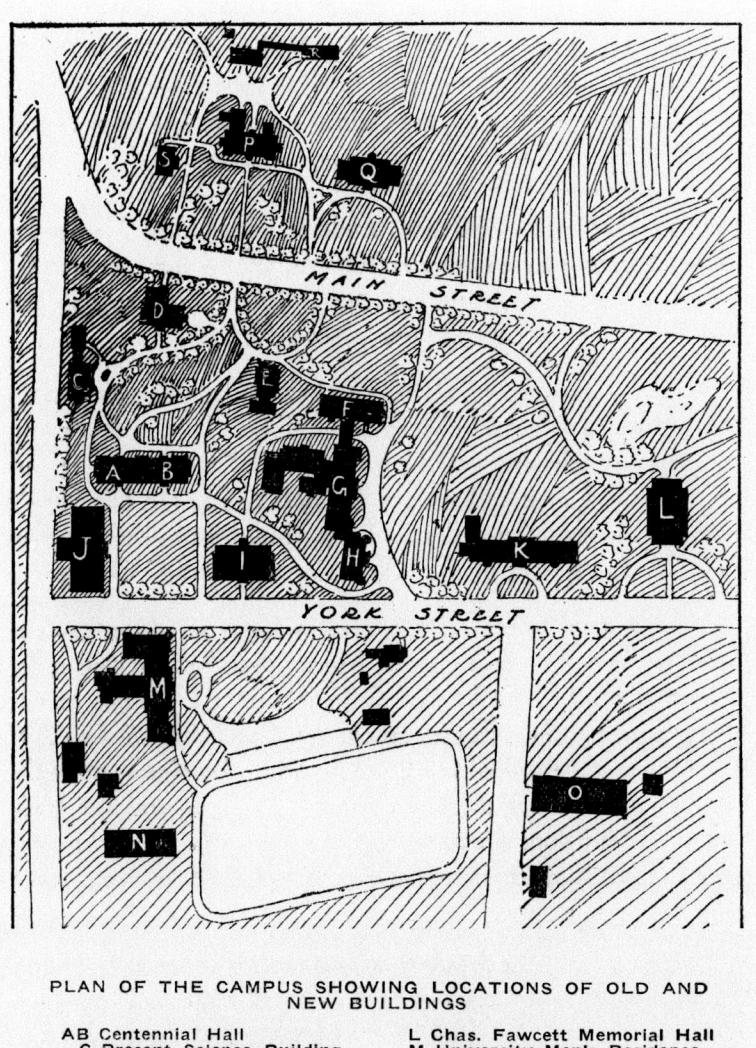

PLAN OF THE CAMPUS SHOWING LOCATIONS OF OLD AND
NEW BUILDINGS

AB Centennial Hall
C Present Science Building
D Memorial Library
E The President's Cottage
FGH Ladies' College
I Owens' Art Building
J Proposed New Science Bldg.
K Proposed New Women's
  Residence

L Chas. Fawcett Memorial Hall
M University Men's Residence
N Gymnasium
O Skating Rink
P Present Academy Bldg.
Q Proposed New Academy
  School Building
R Barn
S Manual Training Bldg.

Allison Hall, the present University Women's Residence, is too far
removed to show in the above plan

3.22 1929 site plan showing proposed new Mount Allison buildings (J, K & Q)

26. *Mount Allison is Yours* (1928), p. 9. [MAA]

27. *The United Churchman* (October 28, 1931), p. 9.

28. *The United Churchman* (October 28, 1931), p. 2.

29. *Mount Allison Yearbook* (1931), p. 20. [MAA]

on the campus and poorly designed, is particularly handicapped in this way. The Department of Biology carries on its work in a small, temporary building erected five years ago in an attempt to meet the pressing needs of the moment. Unless this condition can be quickly remedied, the excellent work which has been done in these subjects in the past must be seriously curtailed... The need of a new Science Building, designed to meet the University's present and coming needs is imperative.[26]

Designed by Andrew Cobb with associate architects Alward & Gillies of Saint John and Combe and Ryan of Montreal (it was a very specialized building, after all), the "stately and beautiful"[27] new science building was opened to students and staff in October 1931, housing the biology and chemistry departments (Figure 3.24). On that day, after the dedication ceremony, the front door was unlocked in front of the gathered crowd by Dr. R.C. Tait of the Board of Regents, who declared the building "dedicated to the search for truth, in the service of God and man."[28] It would accommodate both departments for many years until the chemistry department moved out in 1967. It was renamed the Flemington Science Building in 1970. Built on land formerly occupied by the president's garden, the new science building completed an academic quad along with Centennial Hall, the Memorial Library and the old science building. The largely stone campus was on its way.

Certainly the most Collegiate Gothic building on campus, the Tudor Gothic styled science building was seen as "harmonizing with the Library" at its inauguration.[29] Noticeably different than Cobb's Neoclassical version proposed only two years earlier, its frontal proportions and internal arrangement did remain somewhat similar. Three-storeys and U-shaped in plan, a 125-feet long central section with an inner corridor and staircases at both ends contained the offices, library and smaller laboratories, while the two 45-feet long end ells contained the main laboratories (Figure 3.23). A large 175-seat lecture theatre with terraced seating and a projection booth anchored the core of the building, along with two smaller lecture rooms, one for biology and one for chemistry.

Faced with red Sackville sandstone, olive sandstone trim and a slate roof, the science building presented a dignified and scholarly face, confidently engaging the quad with its central door below a medieval oriel window and gabled dormer. The side-facing Centennial Hall is perhaps the most pleasing of all. Here, its more staid and horizontal ell walls counterbalance the vertically animated gable end with its

3.23 The science building, main laboratories

angled buttresses, off-centre entry and stairwell window, coping stones and triple chimney at the roofline (Figure 3.25).

Belying its historicism, behind the science building's stone sat a concrete slab floor system over a structural steel frame, while operable steel sashes made up the windows. The paradox of an ancient skin shrouding a fairly modern skeleton speaks to this era, when the spirit of higher education was philosophically and architecturally looking for grounding while still attempting to be progressive in the rapidly changing industrial age. After a lengthy discourse regarding the uniqueness and appropriateness of its Tudor styling, *The United Churchman* of October 28, 1931, praised the splendour of the new building:

Ordinarily a science building looks like a big manufacturing plant and is seldom a thing of beauty. The main purpose of a science building is of course utilitarian in nature and it is a great source of satisfaction to Allisonians everywhere to know that while the new science building is one of the very finest in Canada from a strictly scientific standpoint, yet it possesses most unusual architectural beauty.[30]

Although the aesthetics and architectural scheme were sound, the technical side of the science building broadsided the university. The detailed planning required for the specialized equipment and mechanical vent systems was not fully taken into account at first. It was noted that "It soon became evident that the walls of the building had to be honeycombed with vents for escaping gas, the ceilings decorated with a network of acid-proof sewer pipes, the acid-proof desks and tables equipped with acid-proof sinks, and with gas pipes, water pipes, steam pipes and electric wire pipes".[31] This is when the building committee engaged Combe and Ryan, a firm that specialized in laboratory buildings. With the apparatus and equipment consuming over a quarter of the building's budget, it was wise to bring them in as everything soon fell into place. The sophistication did not, however, translate into a modern expression of science and technology. Look no further than the triple vent stacks at either gable end of the building; the stone-clad triplets with their carved shafts wouldn't appear out of place in an Elizabethan manor from the late 1500s. This was Collegiate Gothic incarnate.

One of the most overlooked structures at Mount Allison is the central heating plant building, now also the home of the university's facilities management. As the

30. *The United Churchman* (October 28, 1931), p. 11.

31. *The United Churchman* (October 28, 1931), p. 9.

3.24 The science building, later the Flemington Science Building (Andrew Cobb with associate architects Alward & Gillies and Combe and Ryan, 1931)

3.25 Science building, southern facade

32. *The United Churchman* (October 28, 1931), p. 18.

33. *The United Churchman* (October 28, 1931), p. 18.

34. *The United Churchman* (October 28, 1931), p. 18.

first university building one passes when entering the town from the Trans-Canada Highway, this imposing example of early-twentieth-century engineering shows that at that time even the most functional of uses could warrant noble design and detail (Figure 3.26). Opened in 1931, the weighty brick powerhouse box with its hip roof, tall arched windows and pilasters expressing the steel structure within was designed by architect and engineer Charles Fowler, whose Halifax-based firm C.A. Fowler & Company was now one of the major architectural offices in the Maritimes. The great stack (with its fine base brickwork) as well as the vast open space of the boiler room speak volumes to the energy and effort that have been heating the campus since the inter-war years.

As opposed to the earlier practice of each building producing its own heat, a new central heating system was anticipated to warm the campus for half the cost. It would avoid the continued swell of a dozen individual flues that "belched forth their heavy soft coal smoke which settled in greasy flakes with cruel impartiality on student and professor alike."[32] It would also allow the temperature to be controlled in all the buildings, especially at night, and would reduce scattered repairs from one building to another.

The central heating plant building was very much a regional collaboration. The contractor was Ambrose Wheeler of Moncton, who also built Moncton High School and Notre-Dame de l'Assomption Cathedral in the 1930s. The Goliath steam furnaces were manufactured just a few miles away by Robb Engineering of Amherst. Whether by sheer effort or the availability of a large Depression-era crew, the heating plant was erected and operational in an incredible three months' time. During the summer of 1931 the campus grounds were "cut all to pieces by trenches about eight-feet wide and from eight- to fifteen-feet deep"[33] and filled with new concrete service tunnels that joined every building to the plant. The October 28, 1931, issue of *The United Churchman* called the whole endeavour "A Great Undertaking Carried Out With Efficiency and Dispatch" that it was "well thought out and executed, and marks a great advance at Mount Allison."[34]

Then came March of 1933. In the midst of the Great Depression, funding was drying up and the last thing the institution needed was unplanned expenses, let alone tragedies. In the afternoon on March 1, the Mount Allison Academy and Commercial College building quickly disappeared in a roar of flames (Figure 3.27). Whether it was caused by an electrical fault in the attic or by arson was never

3.26 Central heating plant building (C.A. Fowler & Company, 1931)

3.27 Fire in the Mount Allison Academy and Commercial College building (the third male academy building), March 1933

3.28 A view of the burned-out Centennial Hall after the March 1933 fire

satisfactorily discovered, but it was not helped by the continuous breeze that day, nor by the dry wood shavings packed within the walls as insulation. Two weeks later on March 17, two of the most important university buildings were lost also to fire as the skies lit up like torches. Given that they were in such close proximity, the old science building (the Old Lodge or McClelan building) and Centennial Hall were almost simultaneously engulfed in flames (Figure 3.28). Beyond the buildings themselves, costly laboratory equipment and valuable university records were lost, as was the university chapel. It was estimated to be $130,000 in damage, with only $83,000 in insurance. After lengthy investigation, the cause of the three fires remained unresolved, and for months the town was gripped by paranoia at the prospect of a local pyromaniac on the loose.

Considering that these fires took place during a period of serious economic depression, the grit and enthusiasm that characterized the response were astonishing. Within a year and a half another Mount Allison Academy building (built of stone this time) rose like a phoenix from the ashes. By November 1933, Centennial Hall was also completely rebuilt, as it was luckily discovered that the fire did not seriously compromise the exterior walls and foundation. As fire had left the old science building "nothing but a smouldering smoking mass of debris",[35] it was not rebuilt. It had been made redundant by the new science building nearby. In the spirit of caution, a sprinkler system was installed in the ladies' college building "that ensures the safety of the precious young lives that are housed there."[36]

Only a few weeks after the academy fire, *The Argosy* of March 18, 1933 reported that "plans for the new Academy are being submitted in considerable numbers to the Principal from the architects. It can be assured … that the new structure will be the latest in school designs, and that it will be the pride of the campus."[37] While Gothic may not have been the "latest" in school designs, the new male academy building—the fourth and final—would certainly become a focus of pride at Mount Allison for many years.

Several proposals were obviously solicited, as a series of presentation drawings of a prospective academy scheme by Wolfville architect L.R. Fairn are in the collection of the Nova Scotia Archives. Fairn's design, dating to March 1933, shows a U-shaped building with a main residential section set between a classroom wing and small chapel (Figure 3.29). The proposed three-storey building used a similar

35. *The Argosy Weekly* (March 18, 1933), p. 3. [MAA]

36. *The United Churchman* (January 31, 1934), p. 2.

37. *The Argosy Weekly* (March 18, 1933), p. 3. [MAA]

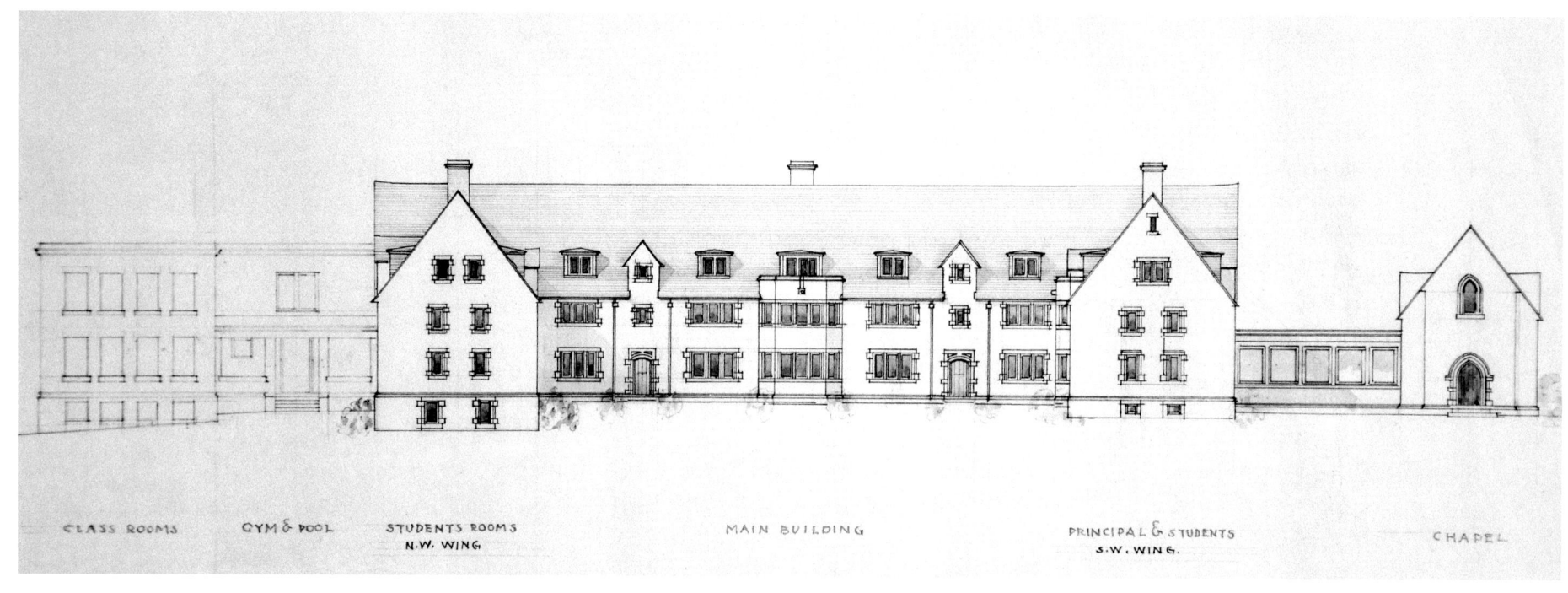

CLASS ROOMS   GYM & POOL   STUDENTS ROOMS   MAIN BUILDING   PRINCIPAL & STUDENTS   CHAPEL
N.W. WING   S.W. WING.

3.29 Front elevation of a proposed Mount Allison Academy building. This scheme had a residential section between a classroom wing on the left and chapel on the right (L.R. Fairn, 1933)

SKETCH OF PROPOSED LAYOUT FOR MT. ALLISON ACADEMY.
SACKVILLE. N.B.
· C.A. FOWLER & CO., ENGINEERS & ARCHITECTS ·

3.30 Architect's rendering of a proposed triad of academic buildings, with the new Mount Allison Academy building as the centre block between two unbuilt buildings (C.A. Fowler & Company, 1933)

3.31 The fourth Mount Allison Academy building, later Palmer Hall (C.A. Fowler & Company, 1934)

fusion of styles to the design that was ultimately selected for construction—Arts and Crafts with Collegiate Gothic.

The successful proposal was a design for a singular academy building intended as the centre block of a trio of similar Collegiate Gothic buildings, extending from its bent arms, all encompassing a common quad (Figure 3.30). The *Mount Allison Record* published two renderings; one showed the residence alone, while another elongated one drew out "the proposed layout complete":

In the background is the Residence, on your right, the Gymnasium and Swimming pool, on your left the Class-rooms. The new Gymnasium and new Class-rooms are dreams of the future—the near future, we hope—They wait, in plan, for someone to put them up as memorials.[38]

History never gave the academy the option of being bookended by the gymnasium and classroom buildings as that "someone" never appeared. It is unfortunate, as judging by the pencil rendering, it would have made a handsome arrangement. Tudor Gothic once again, it was a long run of a building at 251 feet, almost manor-like in appearance but still intimate in detail (Figure 3.31). Some fine stone carving could be found in spots, such as the Mount Allison crest over the main door (Figure 3.32) and the front doorways' flanking stones depicting music, industry, study, boxing, wrestling and football (Figure 3.33). Better symbols for young men of the 1930s couldn't be found anywhere. Faced with the now ubiquitous combination of red Sackville sandstone with olive sandstone trim, it sheathed a three-storey concrete and steel framework confidently referred to as fireproof.

Built on the same site as its predecessors, the fourth male academy building was designed to house 80 students in single and double rooms. Belying the building's Gothic expression, its black and white tiled showers and toilet rooms were deemed worthy of special mention in *The United Churchman*, as "they reflected the ultra modern of present day design."[39] The plan also lodged staff accommodation for 12 professors, the principal's residence, a small medical room, students' living room, reception room, chapel, billiard room, dining room, kitchen, and maids' accommodations. This all-male bastion (save for the maids) would be converted to a women's residence in 1959, the same year it was renamed Palmer Hall. This was

38. *Mount Allison Record* (April–June 1933), pp. 133–34. [MAA]

39. *The United Churchman* (January 31, 1934), p. 15.

3.32 Carved stone details around the central entry door of the fourth Mount Allison Academy building, later Palmer Hall

3.33 Carved stone figure at the entry door arch of the fourth male academy building, later Palmer Hall

3.34 Centennial Hall (renovated by Andrew R. Cobb, 1934)

certainly not on the minds of those laying the cornerstone on July 15, 1933, as Rev. J.A. Ramsay, President of the Maritime Conference of the United Church, declared that "This is a proud day when we can lay the cornerstone of an institution that will give us men."[40]

Its architect was C.A. Fowler & Company, who skillfully created a welcoming front facade with somewhat of a courtyard by bending the plan at 45-degree angles at both ends. Charles Fowler was one of the best architects in the Maritimes, but he also had a serious 'in' with Mount Allison. Labelled "an Old Boy of the School"[41] by the *Mount Allison Record*, in 1933 he was also the new president of the Federated Council of the Alumni and Alumnae Societies. His firm would remain Mount Allison's go-to architects for the next 28 years.

Gutted completely, Centennial Hall was renovated and reopened in January 1934 as an administration and physics building. Andrew Cobb was called on once again, and Centennial Hall kept much of its external form, although the central tower was gone, along with the sizeable Gothic windows with their pointed arches at the second floor (Figures 3.34, 3.36). Throughout the interior offices, laboratories and a lecture hall were laid out, while a much more spartan chapel was designed (Figure 3.35)—with the assumption that a grander one would soon appear:

the Chapel provided in the third floor will provide us with a quiet spot for worship, until some friend makes possible the building of a suitable Chapel, large enough for all the Mount Allison students and faculties to worship together. [42]

Both the fourth male academy building and Centennial Hall were officially opened at a special convocation held on January 19, 1934. Those gathered articulated faith and resilience, and *The United Churchman* account went back to the classics: "It is told in Greek mythology that one Antaeus, when he was thrown to the earth, rose stronger than ever. That is the impression Mt. Allison has given in meeting the unprecedented disaster of last March."[43]

In his address celebrating the opening of both buildings, the Right Rev. T.A. Moore, the moderator of the United Church of Canada, saw them as much more than bricks and mortar; they were metaphors for human achievement:

40. *The Sackville Tribune* (July 17, 1933), p. 1.

41. *Mount Allison Record* (April–June 1933), p. 133. [MAA]

42. *Mount Allison Record* (April–June 1933), p. 133. [MAA]

43. *The United Churchman* (January 31, 1934), p. 2.

3.35 The chapel in Centennial Hall

3.36 Centennial Hall

During these days of supreme interest we are opening for daily service and dedicating to their high purposes, these buildings of stone and iron and cement, whose architectural outlines please the eye and whose interior arrangements make possible the highest efficiency. They will ever declare the ability of those charged with the tasks of coping with herculean difficulties under burdens which were apparently impossible. These buildings will be always a monument to their successful achievement, to a skill in planning, a courage in undertaking, and a satisfaction in completion, which must be a gladness to every friend of Mount Allison, a challenge to every student, and a comfort to themselves. Throughout the lives of many of us these new buildings, which so harmoniously associate themselves with the others which unite to make Mount Allison one of Canada's most effective and efficient educational centres, will be an added adornment to this renowned campus, so dear to the graduates of this Alma Mater, to the people of Sackville, and many others in the nearer Provinces and the distant places.[44]

Each of these Gothic Revival buildings was effectively a revival of a revival, and they speak strongly to the eclecticism of early-twentieth-century Canadian building when British associations were at their apex. Trying their best to look ancient, they were built between the wars at a time when the world was changing faster than anyone could imagine. They remind us that architecture that appears old can often be much closer to our time than we think.

The Depression continued, and no other buildings were begun at Mount Allison until after the Second World War. The university was recovering from the haze of rebuilding and building anew. With a campus that was quite different from that of only a few decades earlier, it was a perfect time to reflect. Sir Charles G.D. Roberts, a pioneer of English Canadian poetry who grew up near Sackville, would often return. Nearing his 80th birthday in 1938, he said of Mount Allison "It is the most beautiful campus that I know in Canada. It is the most picturesque, varied and well-treed campus I have seen in Canada."[45]

The positive air of beauty was short-lived, as the Second World War soon churned up the campus once again. Notwithstanding all the recent erection of 'fireproof' buildings, the second men's university residence building burned on a bitterly cold night in December 1941. Fire spread quickly as the flames shot up through the main stair shaft, and within 15 minutes the building was a blazing

44. *The United Churchman* (January 31, 1934), p. 3.

45. *The Sackville Tribune* (August 18, 1938).

3.37 The second men's university residence engulfed in flames, December 1941

46. Alex Colville interviewed by John Reid, January 20, 1982. [MAA, 8253]

47. *Mount Allison: Today, Yesterday, Tomorrow* (Sackville: Tribune Press, 1943). [MAA]

inferno (Figure 3.37). Four students were killed due to the fire, although many claimed it was a miracle that more didn't succumb as the residence housed 250 men at the time, including 25 RCAF radio technicians in training. The most famous student who escaped the fire was Alex Colville, who had a room on the fourth floor. In a 1982 interview Colville recalled:

I went to bed and went to sleep and my next door neighbour, a guy named Bernie Leith from Cape Breton wakened me, knocked on the door and said "Alex get up! The place is on fire!" I looked out and sure enough I could tell it was bad.... When [my roommate] finally got awake, he started packing stuff and I said "Listen, this is bad. We have to get out, no time to take anything." We were saved, probably by the fact that the old residence had double hung windows, big plate glass windows, and it was usually overheated, and we had developed the habit of removing one whole sash and simply putting it on the floor. Because of this there was lots of fresh air. I persuaded [my roommate] just to forget the suitcase and all that and we went out and down the fire escape.... But we didn't get out any too soon.[46]

The university purchased the Brunswick Hotel in downtown Sackville as a temporary men's residence after the inferno, and it did its job accommodating the displaced students quite well. But like the 1921 temporary gymnasium, the hotel bore the brunt of the overflow of Mount Allison men who couldn't find dorm rooms for far longer than they expected: 17 years.

The first four decades of the twentieth century stood as a continued instance of two steps forward, one step back for Mount Allison, but those resulting single steps forward were jubilant and meaningful. Even during the Second World War, a sense of optimism for the future was embraced, as a fundraising appeal called *Mount Allison: Today, Yesterday, Tomorrow* was undertaken. In its handsome booklet, the campaign confidently stated:

Mount Allison will not stand still; she will go forward or backward. Upon the faith, courage, loyalty and generosity of graduates and friends, the fate of Mount Allison now depends.... Just as the need for Mount Allison's services is greater because of the war, so too, fortunately, is the ability of graduates and friends to contribute generously.[47]

The Allies would win the war, and while Canada shouted for joy, it also breathed a heavy sigh of relief. Life could get back to normal. Through the previous decades Mount Allison expanded and matured, but never veered away from the expectations of what a small university and college campus in eastern Canada should be, and how it should build. This would radically change by the mid-1950s, as the traditional status quo of collegiate buildings would be thrown out like a dishrag. A global catalyst quickly shaped a different identity above the Tantramar marshes. Soon enough they would become consummate Modernists, and the battle would be on.

CHAPTER FOUR

Reacting to the Changing World
1945–1963

For obvious reasons, little was built at Mount Allison during the war years. Scarce resources and dwindling enrollment imposed restraint, but soon enough the wave of returning veterans would not only force the university to build, it would spur vigorous growth during what has been described as a golden age at Mount Allison.

By 1946, returning veterans had swelled Mount Allison's enrollment by 50 percent. At the end of the Second World War, every college and university in Canada underwent a radical shift that forever altered the assessment and experience of higher learning. Discharged veterans, many still in their early twenties, wanted to rebuild their lives, and with the support of a federal government rehabilitation training program, a post-secondary education offered them that opportunity.

The massive influx of veterans enrolling as students overwhelmed Sackville, and many of them could not find adequate housing anywhere. Accommodation was so scarce in the town that some students were put up on bunks in the university gymnasium for the first few weeks of the 1945–46 term. By mid 1945 an army-designed temporary building that could house 60 men in 30 rooms was built to help address the shortage.

An alumni committee led by 1920 graduate William J. West (father of the artist Mary Pratt) had been leading the planning and fundraising for new male housing, replacing the second men's university residence building which had been lost to fire in 1941. The construction of the long-awaited residence was finally started in August 1944, but the war economy soon caught up with the university's finances. Although a building fund cap of $325,000 was seen as enough to complete the residence, by January 1945 the cost estimate swelled to $480,000. By the time it was officially opened in September 1946, the construction cost had exploded to $850,000— over two and a half times the initial estimate. By comparison, the

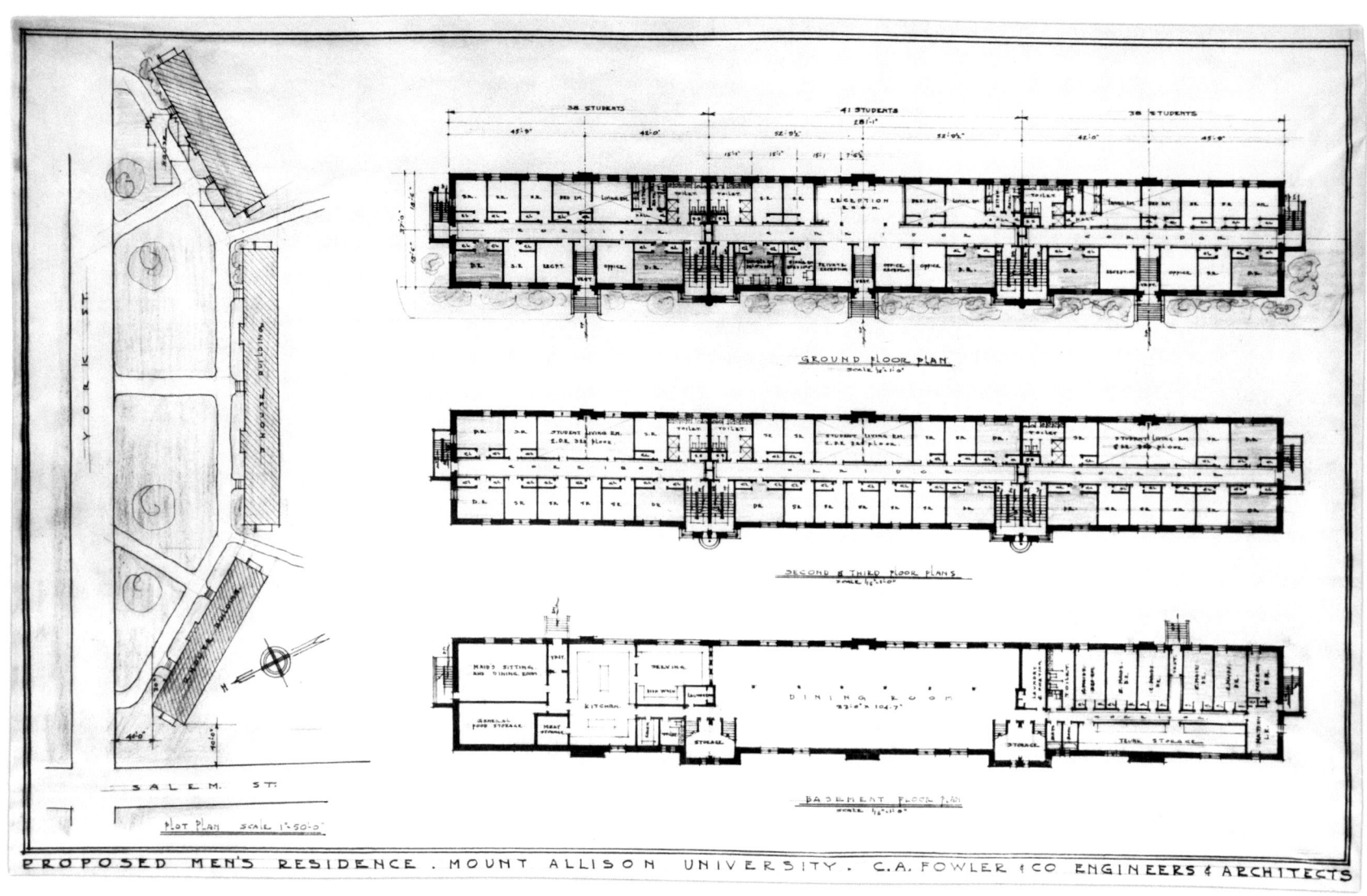

4.1 Architect's plans for a new men's university residence building, later Trueman House, designed as a centre block between two unbuilt residences (C.A. Fowler & Company, c.1942)

4.2 Trueman House men's residence (C.A. Fowler & Company, 1946)

4.3 Trueman House, carved coat of arms of the Allison family atop the main entry. The Latin motto reads: *Vincet Veritas* (truth prevails)

fourth male academy building cost around $125,000 a little over 10 years before, and it was fairly similar in scale, use and material.

Called "a monument to those Allisonians who served in the two World Wars,"[1] the building was initially proposed as the central unit of a group of three similarly-styled men's residences running along York Street (Figure 4.1). As with the proposed arrangement for the triad of 1930s buildings for the nearby academy, only the initial centre block was built. Opened without pomp or ceremony, the new men's residence would be known as Trueman House in honour of Mount Allison's long-serving and recently retired president, Dr. George Trueman, who led the university from 1923 to 1945. Designed by C.A. Fowler & Company, it was built by Ambrose Wheeler, who by now had more than proven himself as one of the most able contractors in New Brunswick, especially if the work involved stone.

Trueman House is a picturesque mass of a building, Tudor Gothic at first glance but with a distinct Art Deco twist through such details as the corner glass block windows at the projecting bays and the faceted stone corbels at the base of the two flagpoles (Figure 4.2). Fowler was obviously feeling less constrained by pure historicism than a decade before, and he seized the chance to insert contemporary details of the day. With punctured windows, varying half-dormers at the roof edge and three distinct entries along the front, the length of Trueman House was adeptly broken down to a human scale. The quality of stone carving and masonry work is excellent throughout, with the red Sackville sandstone employed in a rock-faced random ashlar pattern, inset with smooth olive sandstone sills, lintels and heraldic carvings (Figure 4.3). Plump balconies at each bay taper to a thin drip edge running to the ground.

A large stone-clad, gable-roofed wing named Tweedie Hall was opened a few months after Trueman House was completed (Figure 4.4). The elegant common room was surrounded by large windows on three walls, with a gentle barrel-vaulted ceiling above, two green marble square columns and a green marble-faced fireplace at the end wall. Its real treasure, though, is a substantial mural Alex Colville completed in the summer of 1948 called *The History of Mount Allison* (Figure 4.5). As one of his important early works, the colourful mural sits around the hearth, depicting people in action in front of a backdrop of Mount Allison buildings—some gone, some still standing at the time the mural was painted, including the first

1. *Mount Allison Record* (Fall 1946), p. 28. [MAA]

4.4 Tweedie Hall (C.A. Fowler & Company, 1946)

4.5 Tweedie Hall, interior view. Around the central fireplace is Alex Colville's mural *The History of Mount Allison* (1948)

male academy building, the ladies' college building, the Old Lodge, the second university men's residence and the new Trueman House men's residence that was on the other side of the common wall from Tweedie Hall. As John Reid noted in his *Mount Allison University: A History*, the inclusion of these latter two buildings and their placement at eye level, facing each other, was no accident: "To a remarkable extent the history of Mount Allison from 1941 to 1948 had been dominated by these two buildings, by the burning of the one and the construction of the other."[2] The central figure of a circuit rider and his horse's rear end has been the subject of much speculation over the years, but the person standing next to them is meant to be Charles Allison being converted to Methodism.

Alex Colville considered the mural a major turning point in his career. He didn't want to be "just a landscape painter" and this mural allowed him to work on a single piece over an extended period, and within the physical confines of an architectural space. Colville felt that "painting that mural was really a kind of major thing in my life as an artist."[3]

Tweedie Hall would be the last building that Charles A. Fowler would design for Mount Allison. Although he died in 1950, his firm would remain active on campus under the leadership of his son Charles A.E. Fowler, who joined the firm in 1948 and soon became its principal designer. The younger Charles was educated as an engineer at McGill, followed by architecture studies at the University of Manitoba in the late 1940s. Under its new director, John (Jack) Russell, the Manitoba curriculum had been transformed into the most forward-looking Modernist program in Canada, making it somewhat of a mecca for architecture students from across the country. This progressive outlook would manifest itself soon enough on the Mount Allison campus grounds, but a few more structures rooted in a more traditional style would be constructed in the meantime.

The strain of overcrowding at Mount Allison in the early to mid 1940s was having an impact upon female students as well as the males. A difficult decision was made to close the Mount Allison School for Girls in 1946 in order that its building, now known as Allison Hall, be given over to the university. The school held its final graduation that June, concluding the story of the female academy which initiated the institution's existence in 1854. Some were critical of the closure, but the university was resolute. Allison Hall (ladies' college building/ladies' academy building/

2. John G. Reid, *Mount Allison University: A History* (Toronto: University of Toronto Press, 1984), vol. 2, p. 218.

3. Alex Colville interviewed by John Reid, January 20, 1982.

4. *Mount Allison University President's Report* (May 1947), p. 3. [MAA]

White House) was now an official university residence for women. Later, when Windsor Hall opened in the early 1960s, Allison Hall would no longer be needed as a residence. It would be renovated to accommodate arts department offices and a science lab, bringing its long role in the residential life of the community to a close.

In May 1947, President Ross Flemington optimistically reported that the new mélange of war-wearied veterans mixed with younger, fresh-faced students was working out well, and that they had a tempering effect on each other:

We have students from all backgrounds of life ... fresh from high school days—and from flirting with death and all the horrors of organized evil in the recent war. Living together here has been good for both. There has been no cleavage between Veteran and non-Veteran. The idealism and enthusiasm of those just out of school has helped to drive out the cynicism and skepticism, the bitterness and sadness of the Veteran—and the latter's experience of life and his seriousness have helped to steady the younger man.[4]

The wave of veterans entering university also had an interesting demographic effect. As well as being older than the freshmen of previous years, many veterans were married, so they could not be housed in the tight, noisy single rooms typical of men's and women's dorms. Housing designed specifically for married students was needed, and needed fast. Normandy Hall and Ortona Hall were quickly built in 1946–47 to answer the need (Figures 4.6, 4.7). Named after battles of the recent war in which Canadian solders had played prominent roles, both residences were built by Ambrose Wheeler of Moncton as simple two-storey wood-frame structures with a subtle Classical tabernacle frame at the main entrance. Containing 16 three-room apartments each, Ortona was sited near Trueman House, while Normandy was built behind the male academy building. They were demolished in 1968 and 1970 respectively, having outlived their purpose.

The empowerment of students during the postwar period was also demonstrated by the acceptance by the university Board of Regents of the 1946 student union proposal for the construction of a new ice hockey and skating arena in Sackville. The union would raise $20,000 for the project in the form of hikes to student fees, while the university would be responsible for the remaining $140,000. While there

4.6 Ortona Hall, a married veterans' residence (Garnet W. Wilson, 1947)

4.7 Typical kitchen inside Normandy and Ortona halls

4.8 Allison Gardens (Cecil Burgess, 1948)

4.9 Allison Gardens, interior view

was great need (the old arena was tired and undersized), the university's postwar debt load was on the verge of choking it financially. A war surplus aircraft hangar was considered but deemed inappropriate and not without its own complications.

Ultimately, the plan proceeded, and in December 1948 a brand new Allison Gardens was opened to great fanfare and on-ice entertainment at a site on Lansdowne Street, behind the present Athletic Centre. The architect was Cecil Burgess of Ottawa, a professional with much experience designing similar Canadian rinks. Due to postwar shortages of steel and skilled labour the building progressed in stages, but the final result was one of the more attractive arenas in the province (Figure 4.8). While its official seating capacity was 1500, at a league championship game in 1953 a Sackville team actually packed 2,459 spectators in the bleachers and rafters. The artificial ice surface was spanned by six massive steel trusses that arched over the ice and held up the roof (Figure 4.9). To the north of the ice surface was a two-storey brick wing with public entrances at each end. A public lounge and bandstand were located on the upper level, while offices, washrooms, a snack bar and another lounge occupied the main floor, with dressing rooms at the basement/ice level.

The main facade of Allison Gardens was a sophisticated arrangement influenced by Streamline Moderne buildings of the era, with their smooth horizontal emphasis, flat roofs and long unbroken surfaces. It was more than just a shell for ice competition, it was a conscious expression of progressive design. Allison Gardens is also memorialized in the Colville mural in Tweedie Hall, where its steel truss and framing are depicted as symbols of modern building. Serving for many dedicated years as a winter home of Mount Allison sports, Allison Gardens was demolished in 2003 and replaced by the new Tantramar Veterans Memorial Civic Centre a few minutes away on town land. For the first time since 1920, the university no longer had its own arena.

Following the closure of the Mount Allison School for Girls in 1946, the Mount Allison Academy and Commercial College suspended operations at the end of the academic year in the spring of 1953. University housing pressures were too great, plus academy attendance was down due to the rise of new regional high schools, and so the academy building became a freshman residence for males. For nearly a century, Mount Allison had functioned as three distinct entities: a college (university), a boys' academy and a ladies' college. Now Mount Allison was one entity, with all the younger pupils gone. Any operational impact that may have resulted from the loss of these two branches was shortlived as the late 1950s saw an exponential growth in student enrollment at the university.

A curious anomaly among the campus's buildings is the former Animal Pathology Building, now known as the Bennett Building (Figure 4.10). Designed, built and paid for by the Federal Department of Public Works, it was originally a government lab on the site of the Old Lodge/McClelan Science Building. Intended for the study of animal diseases related to Maritime agriculture, it opened in January 1956 and was aquired by the university several decades later. What is strange about the building is not that it is clearly trying to emulate the 1931 science building it faces (Flemington), or that instead of stone it is made of pink concrete/stucco faking masonry, but that it is such an unabashedly Gothic Revival building designed and constructed in the midst of the great Modernist wave of the 1950s. Through its Tudor styling, steep roof, corner edge parapets and gabled dormers, the Animal Pathology Building would be the last project emulating ancient architecture on campus—at least until the turn of the new millennium when some designs tried, but never succeeded.

Reminiscing about the early days of his Mount Allison career, English professor Dr. Lloyd Duchemin recalled that the 1950s were almost a golden age in Sackville, save for the built landscape (which was about to change):

Mount Allison was not a garden of Eden of course, but if any Canadian university rather nearly approached that paradisal condition, it was ours. The teaching, the scholarship, the standards, were of a high order, the product of a long and excellent tradition. We had all this, and yet we were poor, some of our buildings were falling apart, our facilities were fragile, almost non-existent …

Through the loyalty and devotion of Alumni and friends of Mount Allison, the University began to rebuild itself physically. From generous people like the Avards and the Bennetts, the process of renewal had its first impetus. Then others seized the initiative, and Mount Allison as we now know it arose in its new splendor.[5]

In 1957, only 14 permanent buildings were in use at Mount Allison, which had a student body of 1100 (incidentally, a 79 percent increase from the enrollment in 1950). By the fall of 1969, the university would possess 30 buildings for 1330 students—essentially doubling the architectural presence in number alone, not to

5. "In Retrospect," in *Mount Allison Record* (Spring/Summer 1974), p. 10. [MAA]

4.10 The Animal Pathology Building, now the Bennett Building (Federal Department of Public Works, 1956)

mention that many of those 30 buildings would be brand new, and modern in style and spirit. This boom period coincides with similar building and enrollment expansion at universities across Canada, with most following modernist approaches in their architecture. To give context, total post-secondary enrollment in Canada increased more than fivefold between 1951 and 1970, from 91,100 to 475,700; so one can imagine the physical pressures on university facilities to grow.

Although American universities were tenacious supporters of the eloquent Collegiate Gothic style, they were also the first to let it go. When Hitler's regime closed the legendary German Bauhaus school in 1933, many of its architecture professors took flight to the United States, bringing with them their fierce conviction in collective change and faith in the gospel of Modernism. Walter Gropius's presence at Harvard combined with Mies van der Rohe's teaching and new campus design at the Illinois Institute of Technology in Chicago were game changers. While Canadian universities were slower to grasp the Modernist aesthetic, its influence gradually asserted itself, and Mount Allison helped lead the way in eastern Canada during the late 1950s. Dalhousie University never quite adopted Modernism for its new buildings until the mid-1960s, and while the University of New Brunswick made a few experiments with the new approach, by the early 1960s it was committed to a red brick Neo-Georgian style that would not have looked out of place a century and a half earlier. St. Francis Xavier in Antigonish was taking a similar path.

Traditional building approaches are often difficult to relinquish, as it is easier to return to the tried and true than to embrace the experimental. But the time had come at Mount Allison to make a conscious architectural break with the past; not only because so many other universities were doing so, but because it made sense financially, socially and culturally. The art of carved stone was disappearing as craftsmen aged and costs escalated, and the postwar world was eager for a new physical expression—one that looked ahead, not behind. It was no longer the era of sailing ships, but the time of Sputnik.

As the decade progressed, New Brunswick strived to become modern and to be part of a forward-looking Canada, and Mount Allison and its administration were primed for the journey. The province's economic progress during the 1950s created an aura of technical confidence that found expression in massive infrastructure projects, such as large hydroelectric dams and power plants along the Saint John River, the new Trans-Canada Highway linking New Brunswick with the rest of the country and the enormous Canadian Forces Base Gagetown at Oromocto, with its hordes of new Modern buildings and novel site planning.

Canada first began to witness broader currents of Modern architecture on the West Coast, primarily in the Vancouver area. Internationally respected architects designed with a strong sense of landscape and sweeping form, akin to Frank Lloyd Wright who explored open space and the organic nature of architecture. His Cartesian opposite, Mies van der Rohe pursued a purist, rectilinear style that exploited the new language of gridded curtain walls with fields of plate glass in metal frames. In the 1950s, the impact of these two architectural masters was enormous, and the sensibilities they fostered soon travelled eastward to the Maritimes. A few Canadian Modernist pioneers also had an influence on these changing sensibilities. Jack Russell's teaching at the University of Manitoba combined with his private practice was enormously influential, as was the innovative work of Peter Dickinson and John B. Parkin in Toronto. Canadian architecture began to seriously consider questions of context, material and function as opposed to making a modern program fit into an antique-styled envelope.

Reducing ornament and allowing function to govern became a firmly entrenched Modernist rule. Architects rejected ornamentation almost completely, at the same time embracing innovative technology and dramatic materials such as steel, aluminum, plate glass, concrete block and plastics. A number of noteworthy structures throughout Mount Allison would soon observe a purity of form, quality of material and austere architectural framework that were remarkable for their time and place, let alone polar opposites of what was built only a few years previous. While the University of New Brunswick's campus is not known for innovative buildings, it too dove into the new style with gusto in the 1950s, at least in one instance. The new Memorial Students' Centre opened in 1955 to wide accolades as perhaps the finest student centre in the country. Designed by Stewart and Howell architects of Fredericton, the flat-roofed minimalist brick building was the first in Fredericton to adhere to the principles of High Modernism and break with the stylistic and material rules of the past, and its impression would not have been lost on the decision makers at Mount Allison.

As Mount Allison anticipated the oncoming wave of baby-boom students, it openly welcomed the Modernist approach as a progressive reflection of the changing times. It is enlightening to compare the enormous differences between the

4.11 Physics and Engineering Building (C.A. Fowler & Company, 1958)

4.12 Physics and Engineering Building, auditorium

4.13 Physics and Engineering Building, drafting room

Animal Pathology Building and Mount Allison's first Modern edifice, the Physics and Engineering Building (often referred to as the PEG Building). They were opened right next to each other only two years apart, but they were light years apart in their architectural and philosophical aims. While the Animal Pathology Building was steadfastly cloaked in the Collegiate Gothic (albeit one clad in fake stone), the PEG unapologetically broke with the past with its flat roof, large expanses of glazed openings, exposed concrete block interiors and playful/informal entry sequences.

Officially opened in the summer of 1958, the PEG Building was a C.A. Fowler & Company-designed structure that would have profound consequences for the university (Figure 4.11). With a reinforced concrete post-and-beam superstructure infilled with concrete block, the three-storey 58 feet by 151 feet PEG Building's exterior walls were faced with large areas of continuous window sashes, alternating with horizontal ribbons of composite panels. A one-storey 65 feet by 45 feet main entry pavillion with walls of polished brown granite was set to one side, facing the centre of campus. The building would feature a 204-seat auditorium (Figure 4.12), lecture rooms, numerous laboratories for physics and engineering, offices and faculty labs, a library, machine shop, photo darkroom, drafting rooms (Figure 4.13), a blueprint room and a museum.

The interior was a radical departure from previous models, as the walls were exposed concrete block with the ceilings proudly displaying their open web steel truss structure. Floor finishes ranged from trowelled concrete to terrazzo, 'battleship' linoleum and asphalt tile. Period photographs show the varied responses to the resolutely Modern architectural agenda of the building: a pinwheel entry plan versus a typical central entry of old, the assorted treatment of surface and mass (bare masonry walls and plate glass) and distinct material textures that ranged from smooth planes to textured grids. While perhaps not as dramatic as some Modernist buildings of the day, this honest treatment was quite appropriate for an engineering building where form followed function. The architecture was a visible teaching lesson in itself. As the first truly Modern building on campus, the Physics and Engineering Building's objectives were unmistakable: clarity, precision and logic, all in a mathematically rigorous composition that followed Mies van der Rohe's famous dictum "less is more" (Figure 4.14). Fowler greatly admired Mies van der Rohe's work and welcomed the opportunity to introduce something

4.14 Architectural differences are clearly evident between the modern Physics and Engineering Building (left) and the earlier Centennial Hall (right)

6. Frank Lloyd Wright, "What Form," in *Frank Lloyd Wright: An Autobiography* (Petaluma, CA: Pomegranate, 2005 [1943]), pp. 234–35.

dramatically different to previous buildings on campus, as well as architectural envelopes that got built much faster.

The next great project on campus was more than just a minimalist exercise in Modernism. While it appeared similar in scale and general approach to the PEG Building, the new Avard-Dixon Building expressed a fusion of the Miesian and Wright worlds: ideals of precision and clarity were visible at the extensive window/spandrel curtain wall (Mies), while ornamental possibilities were achieved using light and shadow on sculptural concrete block walls at the eastern end of the main facade (Wright).

In the 1920s Frank Lloyd Wright began to push his ideas about patterned concrete blocks. Utilizing what he called "textile block" as a material challenge, he explained in his *Autobiography*:

What about the concrete block? It was the cheapest (and ugliest) thing in the building world. It lived mostly in the architectural gutter as an imitation of "rock face" stone. Why not see what could be done with that gutter-rat? Steel welded to it by casting rods inside the joints of the blocks themselves and the whole brought into some broad, practical scheme of general treatment, why would it not be fit for a new phase of our modern architecture? It might be permanent, noble, beautiful.[6]

By the 1940s, Wright went from using complex cast block forms to much simpler block shapes, with little or no ornamental relief. This is essentially what we see in the exterior walls of the Avard-Dixon Building: "Shadowall" precast block with recessed corners at both ends, creating a field of strong triangular shadows (Figure 4.15). Sunlight generated an interplay of light and dark along the facade, and the effect was unlike anything else on campus. This dappled pattern was joined by a colourful and geometric Lawren P. Harris mosaic tile mural at the Main Street entrance (Figure 4.16). Harris, a former official Canadian war artist and respected abstract painter, was the head of the university's fine arts department at the time. He designed and installed five exceptional abstract tile murals at Mount Allison in the late 1950s, although only the Avard-Dixon one would survive the ravages of future renovations.

Designed by C.A. Fowler & Company, the three-storey steel-framed Avard-Dixon Building opened in September 1959 as the headquarters of two somewhat

4.15 Avard-Dixon Building
(C.A. Fowler & Company, 1959)

4.16 Avard-Dixon Building, Lawren P. Harris mosaic tile mural at the Main Street entrance, 1959

unrelated departments: geology and home economics. (It was informally, and ingeniously, called the "rock and roll building" by students.) Its rectangular floor plans contained the usual span of classrooms, offices, a library-lounge, and animal and food laboratories, along with a large kitchen and special 75-seat dining room on the top floor. Conscious of the university's cloud of growth, Avard-Dixon was wisely designed so that it could accommodate an additional floor above in the future.

As expected, not everyone in the university community was enamored by the new minimalist building language and raw materials. *The Argosy* condemned the PEG Building as "a blot on our ivy-covered campus"[7] and predicted that it would soon look shabby and dated. In response to these criticisms, a respected figure came to the defense: Alex Colville. When asked about the architecture of the new university buildings and the controversy of the Modern style, Colville told the *Mount Allison Record*:

Our age is generally considered to be producing some of the best buildings of the last two or even five centuries, so it seems obvious to me that we should use the materials, processes, and styles of our time. A university is a living, changing thing; its buildings should reflect this organic character. Thus a campus made up of buildings in several styles is not incongruous provided the trees, the sky, aided by human discretion, can unite the various buildings into a rich but not tedious or static whole.

Also, I believe that our buildings should be well designed and constructed, but that they should make use of the modest materials and techniques which are in keeping with our means ... generally it seems to me that we should class our new buildings as a success.[8]

By the late 1940s, the Memorial Library was already bursting at its seams, having reached its 70,000 volume capacity a mere 20 years after it was built. President Ross Flemington expressed the critical need for a renewed library facility and its centrality to the university's mission:

What is a University? Books. A Library—a constantly growing Library—and we are proud of our Memorial Library here at Mount Allison. A Library that already needs

7. *The Argosy Weekly* (November 15, 1957). [MAA]

8. "An Artist's View," in *Mount Allison Record* (Spring 1959), p. 22. [MAA]

Text within image: FRONT VIEW ~ PROPOSED LIBRARY EXTENSION ~ MOUNT ALLISON UNIVERSITY, SACKVILLE, N.B. ~ C.A. FOWLER & CO., ARCHITECTS

MEMORIAL LIBRARY 1956

A. Kundzins, 15-2-58

4.17 A 1958 architectural rendering of the Mount Allison Memorial Library and William Morley Tweedie Annex (C.A. Fowler & Company, 1960)

an annex for stacks and additional reading rooms. One judges a University by its Library.[9]

9. "The President's Foreword," in *Mount Allison Record* (Spring 1949), p. 3. [MAA]

When the Memorial Library opened in 1927, it housed 15,000 volumes and had a staff of three. By 1960 the collection had grown to 100,000 volumes with a full-time staff of 10. Enter C.A. Fowler & Company once again to design a courageous and efficient addition to the old library, one that was current in spirit and form, sculptural in detail and an excellent example of a thoughtful mid-century Modern addition to an historic predecessor. Officially opened in August 1960, the library's William Morley Tweedie Annex doubled the holding capacity of the existing library and was seen as key to Mount Allison attracting new students and faculty. It was certainly not trying to match its Collegiate Gothic parent, but it was a respectful offspring (Figure 4.17). The Tweedie Annex's volume matched the adjacent Memorial Library's volume up to the start of its roof and used the same red Sackville sandstone for its cladding. A fully glazed atrium joined the new and old sections, with a covered entry stair landing in front. Its sophisticated Mondrian-like pattern of alternating large and small rectangles of glass in deep frames made for a vibrant beginning to the new library. Making the atrium windows seem tame by comparison, the pre-1970 rear wall facing Main Street was peppered with 182 small 8 by 16 inch windows in pairs that danced over the entire facade. The Salem Street facade was half stone and half glass-and-spandrel curtain wall like that used in the PEG Building. The interior of the new annex contained reading/study rooms, rows of book stacks, a periodical room and reference area, all with an economical exposed concrete block wall finish (Figure 4.18).

The uninterrupted front facade of the Tweedie Annex sported a 12-feet tall carved wood relief sculpture by Anne Kahane titled *Sculptural Wall* (Figure 4.19). Kahane was a nationally renowned artist and one of the few Canadian women sculptors at the time. In the late 1940s she studied at the Cooper Union in New York where she began woodcarving, a technique that would dominate her career. A material not often used by sculptors of the era, Kahane's wooden sculptures were dramatic and vigorous, usually depicting the human form alone or in groups. Beyond her many public commissions, she represented Canada at the Venice Biennale, the 1958 Brussels World's Fair and at Expo 67 in Montreal. Her 1961 *Sculptural Wall* was the result of a Canada Council grant given to the university

4.18 Tweedie Annex, book stacks

4.19 Tweedie Annex front facade and main entry with Anne Kahane's 12-feet-tall wood relief sculpture *Sculptural Wall,* 1961

in 1960 for "sculptural embellishment" on one of its new buildings.[10] The monumental mahogany sculpture depicts six interconnected figures and was originally located fairly close to grade near the Annex entrance, making it a dynamic addition to a very social, student-filled spot.

During the 1950s and 1960s, the number of university residences jumped from 4 to 10, but this expansion did not get off to a good start. The 1959 President's Report boasted "with the addition this year of three new residences for men and the Academy for women Mount Allison has a greater percentage of her student body in residence than any other [Canadian] University of a thousand students and over … Residential life should be a very important phase of University life."[11] The three new men's residences he was talking about were Bennett House, Bigelow House and Hunton House (Figure 4.20). The three were virtually identical and all opened in September of 1959 at a combined cost of $700,000. Bennett and Bigelow were built on the site of the former men's residence that burned in 1941, with Hunton a bit farther down Salem Street. For a while they took great strain off the growing demand for living accommodation on campus, as all together they housed 314 male students, but soon enough they would become a burden on the university. C.A. Fowler & Company was the architectural firm responsible for their design, and in this instance its work was not up to the standards of its previous commissions for Mount Allison.

The root of Modern architecture was not, as some critics claimed, a discarding of detail and care. At its finest, Modernism embodied a search for simple qualities that revealed the essence of shelter and human creativity; at its worst, it could be a pretext for poor detailing and the use of cheap materials. Unfortunately the latter ended up being the case with Bennett, Bigelow and Hunton houses, but the architect was not necessarily to blame. In a 2014 interview, Charles Fowler expressed the view that the problems with these three buildings were due to the university pushing bottom-line budgets and tight scheduling requirements that were nearly impossible to meet. In retrospect, Fowler felt he gave Mount Allison exactly what was achievable given the constraints, and that the clients were not prepared to accept an outcome they themselves imposed.

Immediately upon their occupancy, complaints were raised about the noise level between adjoining rooms in these three residences. In the minutes of a 1969 executive committee meeting on men's residences, the members concluded that since

10. *Mount Allison Record* (Spring 1961), p. 20. [MAA]

11. *Mount Allison University Report of the President* (October 1959), Appendix II, p. 1. [MAA]

4.20 Bennett House (centre) and Bigelow House (left) men's residences (C.A. Fowler & Company, 1959). Note the Lawren P. Harris abstract tile mural at the entrance

their completion 10 years earlier, "these residences did not meet the standards of the University."[12] Fowler was asked to undertake a study to see what could be done to bring the residences up to standard. Over that year the Board of Regents went from pursuing a plan of almost completely rebuilding the three buildings down to the foundations and frames, to discussing their complete replacement with new residences, to finally waiting it out and doing more study. By 1972, steps were finally undertaken to reduce heat loss and address noise levels, and to improve the general appearance of the rapidly aging interior and exterior.

By the 1970s, the three residences were labelled as having been "temporary" from their inception, but this was certainly not the case. They only acquired that label in hindsight due to the recurring issues of quality. It seems that Mount Allison did not want to admit that it had underwritten mediocre housing for its students. The three buildings were all substantially renovated in 1981 and 1982 using plans by Halifax architect B. Burtt Barteaux & Associates. On the structural steel frames of the old were added metal mansard roofs, brick masonry veneer, double glazed windows, new electrical and alarm systems, extensive insulation and all the built-in furniture was replaced with moveable units—all completed in an astonishing 10 weeks by local contractors. They now closely emulated the nearby Edwards and Thornton residences—which is not the deepest of compliments. While the initial residences had severe deficiencies and were made of subpar materials, there were some legitimate instances of good Modern design that were lost in the refurbishment, such as Lawren P. Harris's energetic abstract murals below stone-clad entry bays.

Even with these new academic and residential accommodations, the university knew it was running on borrowed time where its buildings were concerned. Only a year earlier, in 1958, it had engaged C.A. Fowler & Company, along with Barott, Marshall, Merrett and Barott architects of Montreal, to create an overall development plan for the inevitable campus growth. They were asked to anticipate the needs over the next 20 to 25 years for a student body projected to double.

The immediate needs listed in the plan were: additional cafeteria and dining facilities for men; at least two more residences for men; at least two, and probably three residence units for women; an addition to the old science building; and a new gymnasium. It was assumed that all of these buildings would be completed by 1962

12. *Mount Allison University Executive Committee Minutes* (December 16, 1969), Appendix IV, p. 1. [MAA]

13. "Chancellor's Address," in *Mount Allison Record* (Winter 1960), pp. 111, 114–115. [MAA]

and would probably cost about $2,750,000 in total. This was seemingly justified, but the Fowler plan would not bear fruit—a far bigger net was about to be cast.

On October 28, 1960, Ralph Pickard Bell was installed as the university's first chancellor. He was perfect for the job in many ways, two of the best reasons being that he was the grandson of Mount Allison's first president and that he was a man of vision and persistence. In his inaugural speech he reminded the audience of the warning of William James, that "the great use of life is to spend it for something that outlasts it." He was indeed going somewhere with this, and in retrospect it was like John F. Kennedy's inaugural presidential address where he challenged America to reach the moon by the end of the decade. Bell asked "what of the future?" proposing that "our objective in the decade of the sixties" should be to raise $7.5 million dollars for new buildings and equipment, and an additional $7.5 million for an endowment fund, allowing the institution to hold and attract to its faculty "the very top level men and women in this most important of all professions."[13]

Replacing the school's 'temporary' gymnasium, which was temporary for over 40 years (Figure 4.21), the new Athletic Centre was the first substantial stand-alone building erected on campus in the 1960s. Located at the corner of York and Lansdowne Streets, it was designed by FENCO (Foundation of Canada Engineering Corporation Limited) with Toronto architects Sproatt & Rolph. FENCO was a considerable Toronto company that also owned a construction branch which built most of Mount Allison's 1960s buildings, including this one. With its opening ribbon cut by Lieutenant-Governor J. Leonard O'Brien on October 28, 1961, the Athletic Centre was the first Mount Allison building that cost over a million dollars to construct.

Proudly displaying the Latin motto on the building's entry portico *Mens Sana in Corpore Sano* (a healthy mind in a healthy body), the centre opened to wide acclaim as the finest athletic facility in the Maritimes (Figure 4.22). This was admittedly a project that was pushed to fruition by long-standing pressure from the student body. The new Athletic Centre contained a 1200-seat capacity gymnasium, dressing rooms, small gymnasium, offices, classrooms and lounge, as well as a 25-metre swimming pool (regrettably built 18 centimetres too long due to a construction error). The six-lane Memorial Swimming Pool is an attractive tiled room enclosed by a sloping roof that curves down opposite the glass block window openings (Figure 4.23).

4.21 The temporary gym, c.1960

4.22 Athletic Centre (FENCO with Sproatt & Rolph architects, 1961)

4.23 Athletic Centre, Memorial Swimming Pool

4.24 Alex Colville standing next to his 1960 mural *Athletes* at the far end of the Athletic Centre lobby

14. Helen J. Dow, *The Art of Alex Colville* (Toronto: McGraw-Hill Ryerson, 1972), p. 82.

Adding yet another Canadian art treasure to the halls of Mount Allison, the Centre's wide lobby contains the Alex Colville mural *Athletes* at the far end (Figure 4.24). His second mural commission from the university, *Athletes* is a monumental tour de force of geometrical balance and composition, with every line and angle related to the whole. A consummate purist, Colville even designed and specified the fluted wall that surrounds the mural and the planter beneath it. The 5 feet by 9.5 feet triptych depicts three athletes on the brink of starting or finishing their physical competition: a swimmer on her starting block, track and field athletes in action and a runner at the finish line—metaphors for the past, the present and the future. As Helen J. Dow observes in *The Art of Alex Colville*, the respect he conveys to the figures is:

based on his penetrating recognition of the profound truth that man himself is created in the image of God. The realization of this truth is the very foundation of his art. This fact gains special emphasis in the Athletes when it is remembered that the form of this painting is a triptych—traditionally an altar painting.… What is more, it presents a strong declaration of the artist's personal conviction about the meaning of life. In its own way, therefore, it is a spiritual statement, and it is on this level that the mural acquires its most profound and universal significance.[14]

Colville's mural and the grand stone porticoed entrance of the new Athletic Centre notwithstanding, it was the onset of a heroic time for university architecture in New Brunswick. Premier Louis Robichaud's Equal Opportunity reforms in the 1960s transformed the social and economic landscape of the province, and one of his greatest triumphs was the establishment of the Université de Moncton in 1963. It was a watershed for the Acadian cultural renaissance of the 1960s and 1970s, as it made the city the Acadian academic and cultural centre. Université de Moncton's yellow brick Modern buildings immediately became the focus of social and educational change in New Brunswick's francophone circles. It was a coming of age expressed in architecture.

While the Université de Moncton's collection of 1960s buildings boldly embodied the progressive courage of the era, the University of New Brunswick was transforming its campus as well. While the Modernist line was sidestepped by red brick Neo-Georgian buildings that were preferred by its president, the Fredericton campus grew by 25 new buildings during the 1960s, tripling in size in a decade. A sister University of New Brunswick campus was built from scratch in Saint John as well, opening at its Tucker Park site on the outskirts of the port city in 1969. Unlike the main campus, UNBSJ's built landscape around a spacious grassed courtyard donned clean, Modern buildings clad with yellow brick and white precast concrete.

Much of this post-secondary advance was due to the momentous Deutsch Commission Report of 1962 that examined the funding of higher education in New Brunswick. Although it said little about Mount Allison directly, the report's recommendations would guide its development right up to the present day: that "Mount Allison continue, for the foreseeable future, its announced policy of development as an undergraduate liberal arts college of limited enrollment."[15] Of an equal, if not greater, consequence would be the commission recommending a tripling of its annual provincial grant to nearly $240,000, along with $650,000 to be spent on capital projects over the next five years. The financial floodgates opened, liberating the university to an incredible degree.

This all coincided with a faculty-led "study of the idea of excellence at Mount Allison."[16] In May 1962, the Mount Allison Faculty Association released a report that "was conceived not as an exercise in abstract idealism, but as a blueprint to be presented by the faculty association to the President, the Faculty, the Senate, and the Regents of Mount Allison."[17] The vast majority of faculty members participated, with much of the report's content relating to coursework, teaching and class numbers, but it also contained a section regarding "Physical Environment":

The physical environment of a university community affects the thoughts and actions of its members. The surrounding complex of natural and man-made features may be thought of as a silent but continually communicating teacher; what is communicated may be orderly or chaotic, beautiful or ugly, life-enhancing or life-demeaning. A Mount Allison aspiring to excellence must give close attention to the planning and maintenance of buildings and grounds, not out of vanity and materialism, but out of the conviction that people, and particularly young people, are significantly moulded by their surroundings.[18]

15. *Report of the Royal Commission on Higher Education in New Brunswick* (Fredericton: Government of New Brunswick, 1962), p. 100.

16. *The Idea of Excellence at Mount Allison University* (1962), p. i. [MAA]

17. *The Idea of Excellence at Mount Allison University* (1962), p. i. [MAA]

18. *The Idea of Excellence at Mount Allison University* (1962), p. 55. [MAA]

4.25 Windsor Hall women's residence (Gordon Adamson and Associates, 1963)

4.26 Main entry section of Windsor Hall, with the end of the 1934 Palmer Hall to the left

4.27 Windsor Hall, main floor reception rooms

In 1961, Sidney A. Windsor, an early-twentieth-century alumnus of Mount Allison, wanted to bestow new women's residences for the campus. He never lived to see them erected, but the Windsor Foundation he established before his death made sure that they materialized, made possible by the largest single gift the university had ever received up to then. Windsor Hall opened in September 1963, while Harper Hall and their connected Jennings Dining Hall both opened in September 1965. Now a co-ed residence, Windsor Hall originally housed 220 women in single and double rooms, while Harper accommodated 156 women in single rooms.

Windsor Hall was unlike any other building constructed at Mount Allison up to that point. The large residence was functionalist, flat-roofed, stocky and clad in brick (Figures 4.25, 4.26). While the brick was intended to have been a sympathetic colour match to the adjacent Palmer Hall, it did not succeed as well as hoped. Five floors in height and 58,000 square feet in floor area, the top three levels contained typical residence rooms, the main floor had reception rooms and lobbies (Figure 4.27), while the lower floor had a recreation area.

Sawtooth in form along its main pedestrian facade, with sparse punched windows and spandrel panels throughout, Windsor Hall embodies a simplified Modernism that is tentative and prudent, expressing a need to be inward-looking. No external flourishes or ornament were to be found, supplanted instead by bare surface texture and straightforward treatment around openings. It was a steadfast brick mass, expressing its role as a secure home for Mount Allison's female students. As necessary as this was, the hall's social connection with the street and community are less than perfect. The most progressive feature in the residence was actually the communal art and designer furniture (sadly now gone): metal side chairs and sensuously upholstered "bird chairs" by Harry Bertoia, along with round tables and executive chairs by Eero Saarinen. Important, original Canadian art hung on the walls, such as work by Molly Lamb Bobak, Lawren P. Harris and Charles Comfort.

The 1959 change of Palmer Hall into a women's residence combined with Windsor created a female residential village at this location, counterpointed by the equivalent male version on the other side of campus through the assembly of Trueman, Bennett, Bigelow and Hunton houses.

4.28 Architect's study model of Harper Hall women's residence (left) and Jennings Hall women's dining hall (Gordon Adamson and Associates, 1965)

19. *Mount Allison University President's Report* (1963–64), p. 3. [MAA]

20. *The Argosy Weekly* (November 5, 1965), p. 3. [MAA]

21. *The Argosy Weekly* (November 5, 1965), p. 3. [MAA]

The completion of Windsor Hall served to push the envelope further for housing the university women. The 1963–64 President's Report declared, "At the official opening of Windsor Hall ... the [Windsor] Foundation would welcome proposals from the university for a second residence and a dining hall to complete the provision for all the students."[19] Mount Allison could not ignore such a good offer, and soon enough a twin to Windsor grew up right beside it (Figure 4.28). Immediately after its opening on Founders Day, 1965, *The Argosy* reported that Harper Hall was a tremendous success, even surpassing the quality of Windsor Hall:

The comforts and conveniences of Harper are unparalleled. It is a residence which consists completely of single rooms, each beautifully compact and yet spacious. The furnishings, not only of the rooms, but the lounges on each floor, plus T.V. room, and downstairs lounges and library are extremely tastefully decorated. Fully carpeted halls are just another touch of elegance which makes Harper more than merely a residence.[20]

The same article glowingly praised the adjacent Jennings Hall (Figure 4.29), the gigantic 500-seat capacity women's dining hall opened the same day as Harper Hall:

The carpets, upstairs lounge, and wide staircase leading to the dining area gives one an immense feeling of elegance. One feels as if one is dining out instead of eating in a university Dining Hall. There are tunnels leading from all three girl's residences to the Dining Hall, and considering the climate of Sackville what could be more appropriate?[21]

4.29 Jennings Hall women's dining hall, interior

These three buildings were designed by Toronto's Gordon Adamson and Associates, one of Canada's most highly acclaimed architecture firms at the time, and one that made a major contribution to the advancement of postwar Canadian Modernism. Adamson opened his practice in 1934, and while his earlier buildings were usually Neo-Georgian in style, during the early 1940s Modernist traits began to take over his work. By the mid-1950s the Adamson office had become one of the dominant forces in Canadian architecture, noted for its focus on design excellence and technical expertise. Minutes from the 1960 Board of Regents meetings show that objections had started to arise about the work of C.A. Fowler, especially after the problems with the beleaguered male residences, leading to the firm's dismissal as campus architects.

Around this time, university Chancellor Ralph Pickard Bell had met with Adamson in Toronto. Inspired by a visit to Adamson's recent women's residence at the University of Toronto (Margaret Addison Hall), Bell encouraged the Board of Regents to see the work in person and to engage the firm's services. In January 1961, several members of the board travelled to Toronto and "felt that the Architects ... had done a very fine job and were much impressed by the members of the firm whom they had met."[22] By February, Mount Allison had hired Adamson. At the time it had just won its second Massey Medal for architecture for the Kipling Collegiate Institute, the highest such award in Canada. While its Mount Allison work may not rank at the same level as its award-winning projects, the buildings it designed for the campus were of their time and have survived more than half a century of use—in and of itself a strong compliment.

Not leaving the hungry young men out of the picture, McConnell Hall was erected for them in 1963, the last C.A. Fowler project at Mount Allison. It contained a kitchen, two distinct meal halls and a smaller banquet room (Figure 4.30). Directly connected to Trueman House, it was named after the McConnell Foundation which funded the hall's construction.

The postwar years had been ones of radical change for Mount Allison. By 1963 finances were finally on a solid footing, Modern architecture was endorsed by the institution, curriculum was strengthened, enrollment was up and the first of the baby boomers were starting to trickle in. But little did this prepare Mount Allison for the next decade.

22. *Mount Allison University Executive Committee Minutes* (January 17, 1961), p. 2. [MAA]

4.30 McConnell Hall men's dining hall (C.A. Fowler & Company, 1963)

CHAPTER FIVE

Turning the Campus Inside Out
1963–1980

University presidents come and go, and while they all contribute to the campus legacy, there are some whose vision can be truly transformational. Laurie Cragg, Mount Allison president from 1963 to 1975, was one such visionary, and his trust in a small Toronto architecture firm forever changed the face of both the university and Modern architecture in New Brunswick. Cragg was instrumental in establishing the blueprint of the present-day Mount Allison, and he did so by engaging and empowering the Ontario-based firm of Brown, Brisley & Brown. Cragg had tremendous faith in both the firm's insight and its pedigree. It was a venerable, family-based company that had demonstrated a dedication to finely-crafted buildings, but admittedly it had little experience in the area of campus planning; for more than two generations its specialty had been designing churches.

The son of a British Royal Engineer posted to Canada, John Francis Brown established his own architecture firm in Toronto in 1891, specializing in the design of churches for clients throughout southern Ontario. In 1924 his son Bruce joined him, followed by Ross Brisley in 1942. The firm continued to build a reputation for its church designs, often in the Neo-Gothic style. In 1958 Bruce's son Douglas came in as the third generation of architects in the family, bringing with him a more contemporary design sensibility, and the firm became known as Brown, Brisley & Brown.

F. Bruce Brown was a charismatic figure who served in Siberia with the Canadian Expeditionary Force during the First World War. After the war, he followed his father's trade, graduating from the University of Toronto School of Architecture in 1923, followed by a year of scholarship study at the Fontainebleau School of Fine Arts in France. As an architect he was prolific, designing over 100 churches

5.1 McMaster Divinity College and chapel (Brown, Brisley & Brown, 1960)

5.2 McMaster Divinity College, chapel interior

during his career. His magnum opus in Ontario, however, was his 1960 design for McMaster Divinity College and its chapel in Hamilton (Figures 5.1, 5.2).

With a design rooted in Eliel Saarinen's groundbreaking 1949 Christ Church Lutheran in Minneapolis, Bruce Brown's college and chapel building was a combined study/worship facility that blended monumentality with the sublime poetry of craft, material and light. Dramatic and powerful, it was lauded by Stanley Porter in his sermon, "Pillars of Worship," celebrating the building's 50th anniversary:

It is a building beautifully designed by Bruce Brown, the architect. Its perpendicular style has a sense of grandeur, but is also ideally suited to creating a worshipful experience. The windows on the sides—with colored pieces of glass numbering the congregations in the Baptist Convention at the time of its building—filter light through in a spectacular array as we worship during the changing seasons.

Our chapel is also a thing of beauty in itself—it is full of beautiful and artistically designed features ... some of them with no other apparent use—and none is needed—than that they are beautifully created to enhance worship.[1]

During the period of the McMaster Divinity College project, Laurie Cragg was a chemistry professor at McMaster University and he was taken by Brown's design. When Cragg became the president of Mount Allison he approached Bruce Brown about designing a new chapel for the university. A few concepts for such a building had been percolating a while, as acknowledged by the President's Report of October 1958: "... the Chapel may at long last be an actuality. It has for years been a dream of Allisonians."[2] When Cragg discussed the chapel with Brown, Brisley & Brown in early 1963, the architects realized that a chapel ought not be designed until a broader plan for the future of the campus was known. Brown, Brisley & Brown saw it as logical to do a full analysis of the existing landscape, pathways, parking and building stock of Mount Allison, realizing that much of it was approaching the end of its functional life. The gradual accretion of buildings over the past century resulted in almost all being individual buildings accessed from perimeter streets and lanes rather than off the central quadrangle as they are today. Bruce Brown convinced Cragg and the administration to engage his firm for a full campus master plan—an exercise that had already been undertaken by C.A. Fowler & Company only a few years earlier, though its findings were gathering dust.

1. Stanley E. Porter, "Pillars of Worship," in *McMaster Journal of Theology and Ministry,* vol. 12 (2010–11), pp. 129–130. Transcript of sermon delivered in the Nathaniel H. Parker Chapel of McMaster Divinity College on September 22, 2010, to commemorate the fiftieth anniversary of dedication of the chapel on September 22, 1960.

2. *Mount Allison University Report of the President* (October 1958), p. 15. [MAA]

3. Douglas Brown interviewed by John Leroux, February 12, 2014. [MAA, 2014.60]

Implementing a complete re-envisioning of the aged campus would be an incredibly bold thing for the administration to do, but it was a bold and audacious time for universities. Vast physical changes were happening at every university in New Brunswick. In fact, there was great expansion underway on most other campuses throughout Canada. Many campus designs were based on the model of pedestrian precincts enclosed by vehicular road, such as the new postwar campuses at Waterloo, Guelph and Trent. The spirit of the era was geared to rejuvenation and dominated by an 'out with the old and in with the new' mentality.

Brown, Brisley & Brown believed that a large central courtyard should become the nucleus of a new pedestrian-friendly arrangement. But the Sackville campus's disparate infrastructure was viewed as being an impediment to major campus reorganization and its potential benefits. Douglas Brown, in particular, remembers:

The one thing we did for them that probably was more important than any of the buildings was to create that master plan and basically turn the campus inside out. In other words, from being peripherally entered buildings individually in spots, to have them entered from the centre of campus. We felt that the existing buildings weren't related; entering them was problematic ... We wanted to bring the thing together. We wanted to use materials that had been used in the older [stone] buildings because we knew some of them were staying there, and there would be new buildings.

We all wanted the kids to have a place to walk from one place to another. I don't know whether we did it or not, but I know that before they put the exterior walkways in there we were going to go up in the highest place we could and wait for the first snowfall and take pictures of where the footprints went so we could understand where the walks should go.

But that was the thing that pushed it, we wanted to create that central campus space and we wanted to maintain the use of the materials so that they wouldn't fight with the old buildings. At that time we didn't know which ones were for sure going to stay there and which ones weren't.[3]

The university agreed, and by the end of the 1960s Brown, Brisley & Brown had not only designed and executed a colossal overhaul of the site plan and landscape of Mount Allison, it had also designed most of the new buildings in a Modern,

5.3 Scale model of the Mount Allison campus showing the existing buildings and the proposed Chapel (Brown, Brisley & Brown, 1963–64)

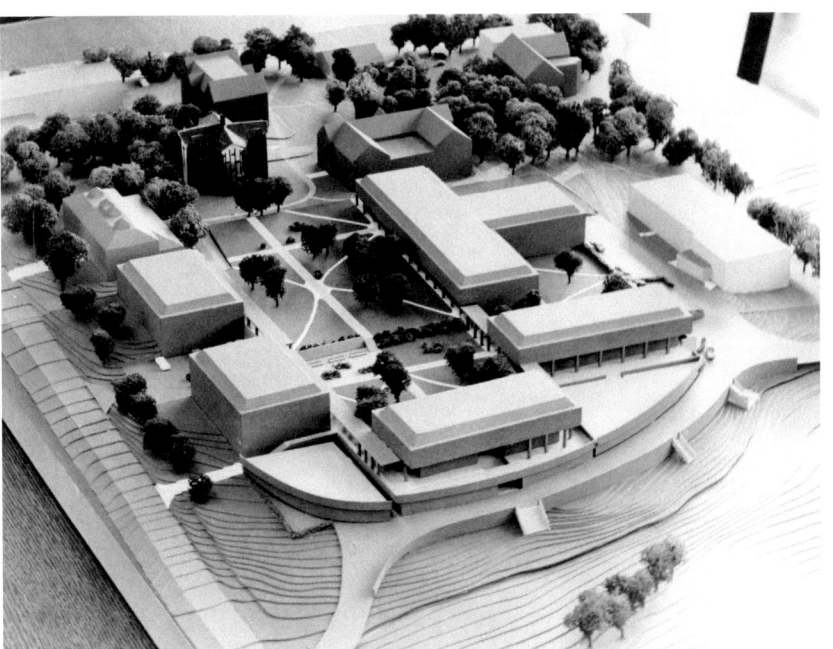

5.4 Scale model of the Mount Allison campus showing the initially proposed new buildings around the central courtyard and open colonnades (Brown, Brisley & Brown, 1963–64)

4. Douglas Brown interviewed by John Leroux, February 12, 2014.

rational style that employed the campus's ubiquitous red sandstone shell. These included the fine arts building, the Conservatory of Music building, the chemistry building, the university library, a number of residences and the remarkable university chapel. Its final building on the Mount Allison campus, the Harold Crabtree Arts Building, would complete the family a decade later.

Before today's great lawn and central quad existed, the space was filled with parking lots, hydro poles and garbage cans. Much of the responsibility for configuring a new organizing scheme for this space was put in Douglas Brown's young hands. He recalls building study models and working on the master plan probably more than anybody else in the office, with Bruce Brown undertaking the task of negotiating with the decision makers at the university:

We built a scale model of the centre section of the campus, right to the streets on either side, which I worked on a lot (Figure 5.3). And at that time there were still big white framed buildings across the hill and on top of the hill. [Gordon Adamson] did a scheme for a chapel right on the brow of the hill where the Arts and Library buildings are now, and it hadn't somehow sat properly with people. So we thought if we were going to put a chapel in there we'd better know where it's going to go and what it's going to do in relation to other buildings.

As it was a United Church college background, and that was very important to a good many people at that time, we felt that the chapel should have a fairly central position. That was part of the reason we created that [cross-shaped] form, so that you could come into it from any one of three sides. The main entrance would face the main campus looking down towards the hill… There had been talk of moving the chapel off campus into one of the side areas, but we felt this was the right place for it.

At the same time, we had the blocks laid out very close to what's there now, where the chemistry building is, where the arts building and the library are and the connection to the hill (Figure 5.4) … The Owens Art Gallery was staying, and the fine arts building at that time was naturally going to go somewhere adjacent to it.[4]

Presented to the university in the fall of 1963, Brown, Brisley & Brown's plan focused on creating intimate and human-scaled spaces. In part, this was accomplished by linking the new buildings from the centre rather than from the perimeter, with a proposed grassed quad becoming the heart of the campus. In aiming to unify the university, Brown, Brisley & Brown recommended a memorable open park that was welcoming and comfortable, while maintaining a spirit of historic collegiality and facilitating efficiency of pedestrian movement. Douglas Brown recalls this as being the core of the vision the architects sought to achieve, that "this was to be what people thought of when they thought of Mount Allison University."[5] The firm's master plan was approved in principle by Mount Allison on October 1, 1963,[6] but was frequently refined as the university administration expressed concerns about "the treatment of the brow on the hill"[7] and about ensuring "a broad vista from the central campus."[8]

The architects' vision sought to generate something that did not exist: an arrangement that would effectively alter the life of the university through fostering a sense of unity throughout the campus. Importantly, the buildings Brown, Brisley & Brown eventually designed for the campus were not cookie cutter duplications, which was a common problem on many 1960s campuses where Modernist functionalism could easily overextend into banality. Outside of the recurring use of red sandstone cladding, Mount Allison's new buildings were surprisingly diverse in their exterior forms and detailing. Function was implied in form. The architects' decision to not repeat themselves had precedent in their ecclesiastical work, where clients inevitably wanted each church to be a unique expression of a congregation's faith.

The Brown, Brisley & Brown projects are remarkable in the way they embodied the qualities of the new Mount Allison to come, and in how those qualities contrast with the campus visions proposed by Fowler and Adamson. While the latter focused on a pluralism of new "commonplace" materials, Brown, Brisley & Brown's consolidation retained tangible elements of the campus's past—namely, the persistence of red sandstone exteriors. Yet by adding a sculptural and expressionist sensibility to each of their overall forms, the buildings now sang to one another in their idyllic setting. As its countless church designs testify, Brown, Brisley & Brown cared deeply about establishing buildings as physical presences in the landscape, and in this the dignity of materials was key. The firm's earlier projects often included a fusion of stone, brick and wood under sloping copper roofs, with aluminum framed windows and special fenestration patterns of minuscule repeating windows—and handcrafted sculpture wherever possible.

The architects appreciated the grounding and dignified aesthetic of the reddish

5. Douglas Brown interviewed by John Leroux, February 12, 2014.

6. *Mount Allison University Executive Committee Minutes* (October 1, 1963), p. 2. [MAA]

7. *Mount Allison University Executive Committee Minutes* (March 17, 1964), p. 4. [MAA]

8. *Mount Allison University Executive Committee Minutes* (April 16, 1964), p. 8. [MAA]

9. Douglas Brown interviewed by John Leroux, February 12, 2014.

Sackville stone, feeling that unity among the buildings and their materials would ensure a harmonized environment. Douglas Brown remembers that his father was keen on the university reopening its quarry that still held large masses of rich red sandstone:

That [stone] defined, to some extent, what you could do with the [new building] shapes and the spaces. My father used to always say "You have a brick building, it's 25 years old, and it's starting to look tired. After 25 years, a stone building just starts to smile." [9]

Although the chapel was the impetus that brought Brown, Brisley & Brown to Mount Allison, its design was actually the third that was presented to the university administration in that period. The first two were by firms that had contributed significant buildings to the campus over the recent past: C.A. Fowler & Company and Gordon Adamson Associates. Although unrealized and little-known, these proposals provide an interesting look at the paths not taken in the architectural development of the campus, chronicling directions that very well could have been taken, proposed by firms that had the ear of the administration and were designing in the reformist temperament of the day.

The 1958–59 C.A. Fowler & Company proposal was for a massive open-plan form designed to accommodate about 500 worshippers under an immense barrel-vaulted roof beam structure (Figure 5.5). The study drawings depict a large coloured mural of Christ and the Apostles that took up most of the exterior's principal facade above the entry doors. This building would have had momentous public presence and coupled well with Mount Allison's tradition of commissioning large murals—although none approaching this scale. In the 1950s and 1960s, rarely was a public building or church constructed without the commissioning of a substantial mural or a prominent piece of public art. A daring feature—hard to imagine in today's context—was the proposal to set the building partially over the swan pond. Too bold, it appears, for those who were holding the reins. The proposal was not well received and C.A. Fowler & Company's design was not pursued.

When several members of the university board viewed examples of Gordon Adamson Associates' university residence work in Ontario in January of 1961, the firm was noted as being "interested in being given an opportunity to design a

5.5 Chapel design proposal (C.A. Fowler & Company, 1958–59)

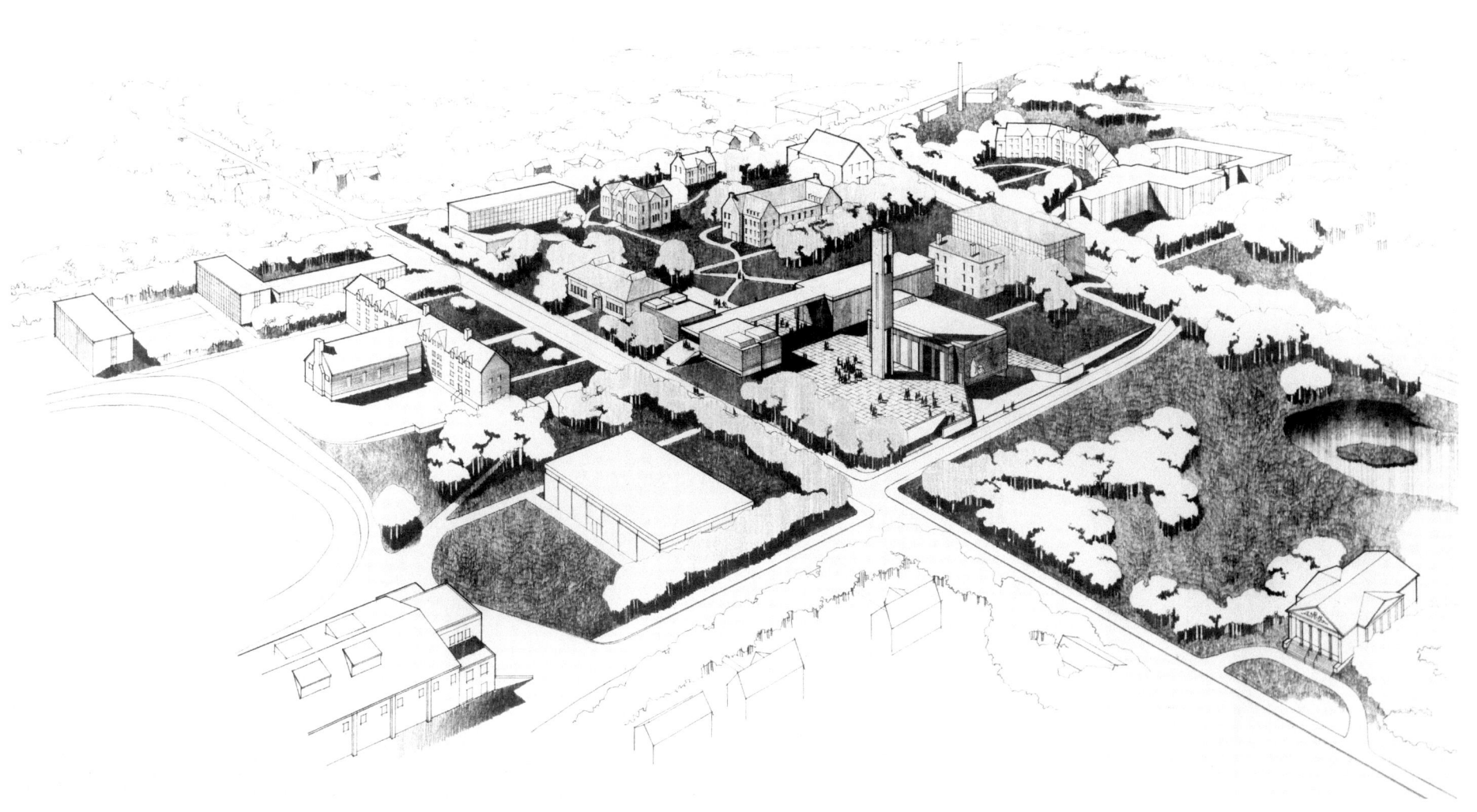

5.6 Chapel design proposal (Gordon Adamson Associates, 1961)

10. *Mount Allison University Executive Committee Minutes* (January 17, 1961), p. 2. [MAA]

11. *Mount Allison University Executive Committee Minutes* (March 21, 1961), p. 4. [MAA]

12. *The Idea of Excellence at Mount Allison University* (1962), p. 57.

13. *Mount Allison University Executive Committee Minutes* (October 1, 1963), p. 2. [MAA]

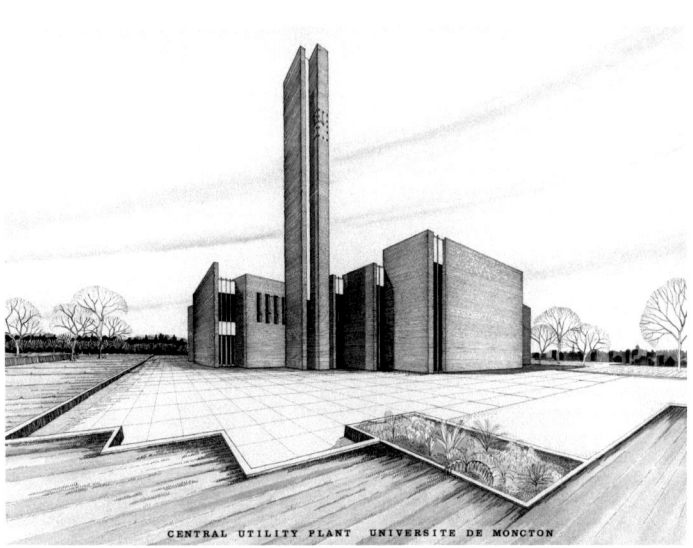

5.7 Université de Moncton heating plant (Alfred Hennessey Architect, 1965)

Chapel for us,"[10] and several of the firm's recent Toronto churches were scrutinized. Liking what they saw, in March 1961 the board moved that Adamson "be asked to prepare preliminary [chapel] sketches for each of the sites, I.E. The area near Main Street and the Home Economics-Geology Building and the Allison Hall area."[11] Pursuing the latter option, Adamson's subsequent chapel plan was an assertive, monumental design that would have stood where the Conservatory of Music building and Allison Hall sat previously (requiring their demolition), and where the current library stands (Figure 5.6). Pervasive in Adamson's design were large hard-surfaced plazas which were in vogue for the front of public and corporate structures at that time, inspired by such projects as Mies van de Rohe's 1958 Seagram Building in New York. Acknowledging the school's religious roots, Adamson's chapel would have dominated the crest of the hill like a figurehead overlooking Sackville below. Similar to Saarinen's Christ Church Lutheran, Adamson placed a tall squared tower as the focal point with a rectangular church volume alongside, accompanied by several new and related buildings. Foreshadowing another key piece of Mount Allison architecture (to be planned and built by others) was a tall covered colonnade between the chapel and the rest of the campus. While never built, the spirit of Adamson's scheme found expression nearby at the Université de Moncton in its 1965 heating plant building, designed by Charlottetown's Alfred Hennessey Architect, with its tall buff brick mast that stood for a different type of power (Figure 5.7). It is worth noting that the Mount Allison Faculty Association's 1962 *Idea of Excellence at Mount Allison* report was critical of any new chapel that "commands or overlooks the town." Their suggestion that "its main entrance should be from the centre of campus, and that the chapel should be conceived as a building within the campus"[12] contrasted with the Adamson scheme.

Ultimately, it was Brown, Brisley & Brown's chapel design that won approval. When Bruce Brown first presented a model and drawings of the proposed chapel in October 1963, the minutes record that members of the university's executive committee "were very favourably impressed" and unanimously supported the project.[13] Officially opened in September 1965, the Mount Allison Chapel is not only the most beautiful Modern building in New Brunswick, but one of the most architecturally inspirational as well (Figure 5.8). Its execution of detail is nothing short of immaculate, its material quality virtually flawless. From the character and

5.8 Mount Allison Chapel
(Brown, Brisley & Brown, 1965)

5.9 Aerial photograph of Mount Allison, 1965. Note the new chapel nearing completion at the centre of the campus

colour of the local red and olive sandstone cladding to the joyous blaze of stained glass throughout the interior and the copper-clad roofing and *flèche* on top, the chapel is a marvel. It is also one of the few buildings that feels equally comfortable and intimate whether you are in it alone or in a crowd of 200 people.

The framework of Christian tradition is deeply embedded in this project, though not at the expense of welcoming those from other traditions. Of this, Rev. Dr. Harold Vaughan, Secretary of the Board of Colleges of the United Church and a Regent of Mount Allison, said of the chapel upon its opening:

A chapel in such a setting should rightly take cognizance of certain peculiarities of tradition. It should do this, however, in full awareness of the fact that it has been built at a time when there is urgent need for the reconciliation of men to one another. No recollection of the past must be so emphasized that it will interfere with the re-unification of mankind and the Church. The historic facts which are reflected in the design of the building and its decoration are not intended to be a comment on any other traditions or symbols which are of equal moment.[14]

This welcoming spirit is certainly evident in the work of the architects, but there is so much more at play. While the chapel is unquestionably steeped in a millennium-old tradition of building spaces for Christian worship, its meticulous design and setting allow it to escape the confines of any one religious doctrine and function in that rarefied, mystical realm of pure space and light. The sensation when one enters the sanctuary alone is paradoxical, as it is a space which feels as protective and enveloping as a womb and yet as expansive as the heavens. As the celebrated American architect Louis Kahn said in 1961: "A great building, in my opinion, must begin with the unmeasurable, must go through measurable means when it is being designed and in the end must be unmeasurable."[15]

Because it was meant to be the focal point of the university, the chapel's shape was purposefully non-rectangular; the architecture needed to be both a spiritual and physical hub of the new campus (Figure 5.9). The choice of a cruciform shape, combined with the compact plan, encouraged a lofty proportion, pushing upward to create a feeling of sanctified space. Bruce Brown held that "the horizontal relationship is man to man and the vertical relationship is man to God."[16] The

14. "The Purpose and Uses of this Chapel," in *Mount Allison Chapel* (1965). [MAA]

15. Louis Kahn, "Form and Design," in *Louis I. Kahn: Writings, Lectures, Interviews* (New York: Rizzoli, 1991), p. 117.

16. Douglas Brown interviewed by John Leroux, February 12, 2014.

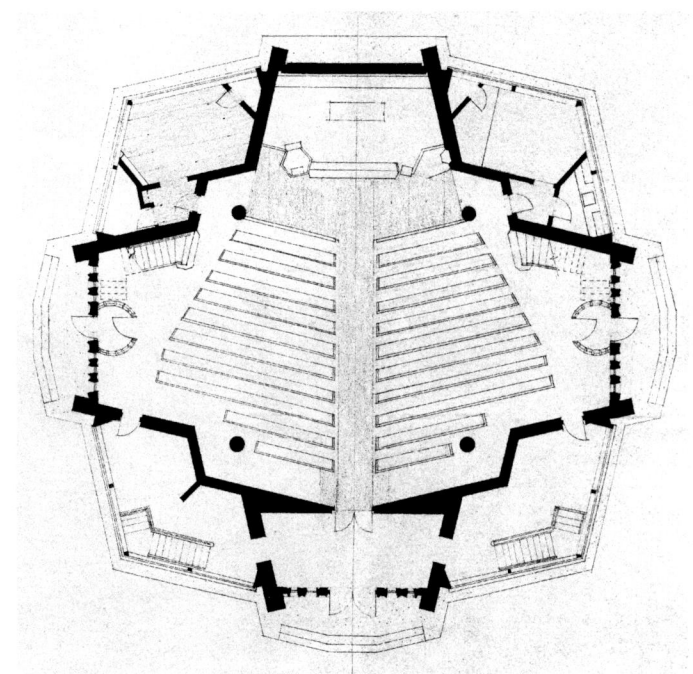

5.10 Mount Allison Chapel, ground floor plan

5.11 Mount Allison Chapel, main entry door and canopy

5.12 Mount Allison Chapel, altar/communion table with reredos behind

5.13 Mount Allison Chapel, reredos and ceiling showing the dimensional stone cross surrounded by stained glass eyelets

Greek cross shape was specifically chosen as it was desired that the chapel could be entered and exited from any direction. It acted as a pivot point for anyone on campus (Figure 5.10). The wall behind the altar was the only branch without a door, a contrast to the direction facing the quad that was the principal entry.

The chapel volume as a whole was made more elegant by the red sandstone walls having a slight taper in plan—a refinement that made the four prominent ends appear narrower and higher than if they were built at blunt right angles. The pattern is repeated at the wood details on the entry doors (Figure 5.11). This conscious link demonstrates the extent to which even the smallest element mattered, upholding Mies van de Rohe's famous architectural dictum that "God is in the details." The four end walls used smooth olive sandstone punctured with a staccato grid of small rectangular windows, a counterpoint to the building's textured red sandstone mass. The gridded form recalls the prominent baptistry window at Coventry Cathedral in England, a Modern masterpiece completed only a few years before.

The interior arrangement of the chapel is a centre-aisled Greek cross leading to a slightly raised chancel. Here a cantilevered stone communion table (Figure 5.12) lies between a painted-steel-bar pulpit on one side and lectern on the other. Upper level balconies sit within three of the four cross wings, one with a large Casavant organ which helps to fill the chapel with music. The chancel wing is open for its full-height with a smooth olive sandstone reredos wall. This wing is the immediate focus as soon as one enters the worship space, with its huge dimensional stone cross surrounded by stained glass drops and offset vertical reveals (Figure 5.13). The building's high ceiling is a *chef-d'oeuvre* of wood detailing, as the perimeter geometry guides the thin wooden slats that all meet at the centre point. Around the outside of the sanctuary are ancillary rooms, including the stone-clad entry narthex, side cloakrooms (one holding the university's *Book of Remembrance*), a small meditation chapel at the northern corner and a vestry at the other. Below the main worship space, a large gathering room occupies most of the basement.

The chapel's structure is articulated by slightly separating the red stone walls from the four concrete columns (each which has a top crest representing an Evangelist). The gaps are infilled with brilliant stained glass, dematerializing the walls as they emphasize the change in direction. These and the large punctuated transept windows (Figure 5.14) encompass an incredible collection of modern jewel-like stained glass, possibly the most moving asset of the chapel. They were

5.14 Mount Allison Chapel, interior view of the north transept window

designed and crafted by Gerald Tooke, one of Canada's top glaziers, and donated by Marjorie Young Bell, one of the university's most generous benefactors.

Tooke's chapel glass is largely abstract, with rich colours in a riot of small patches not unlike a Riopelle painting, although some figurative and symbolic elements can be found within the work (Figure 5.15). The large transept windows employ brilliant pure colour, while the tall column windows employ warm neutrals with some orange highlights. The three transept windows have as their leitmotif "creation" (east window), "incarnation" (north window) and "redemption" (south window). If you look carefully at the windows, you can find elements representing the four Evangelists. Within the glazing, Matthew (southwest pillar) is represented by a winged man, Mark (southeast pillar) as a lion, Luke (northeast pillar) is depicted by a winged bull and John (northwest pillar) is signified by an eagle. Being a building completely in the round, wherever the sun moves throughout the day, sections of Tooke's glass are ablaze with fiery light; the effect on the relatively dark chapel interior is dazzling.

The tactic of using small stained glass squares around a reredos cross had previously been adopted by Brown, Brisley & Brown in 1961 in their design of St. Bride's Anglican Church in Mississauga. The firm often textured its church reredos, and these punctuated holes around the raised stone cross were designed to give it a luminous sparkle so that if one entered the building during the day with no lights on it would still read as a cross on the wall. In this application, Tooke's stained glass windows are effectively points of light, acting like stars which invite you to gaze at the heavens—a perfect effect for a space that aims to evoke the infinite.

However perfect the chapel may seem, no construction project is ever flawless. Sackville resident Jean Cameron—daughter of the long-serving university registrar, Donald Cameron—recounts a peculiar story about the installation of the windows:

On the day that the chapel was dedicated, [Dad's] mother, my grandmother, went to the service. She arrived in time to read through the Order of Service and the explanation about the glass, and she looked closely at the panels. After the service she pointed out to Dad and Dr. Bell that she believed that the glass had not been installed correctly, that the pictorials were adjacent to inappropriate pillars. She was proven correct and two panels were determined to be misplaced. The workmen had to return and take down these two panels and reset those windows ...

5.15 Mount Allison Chapel, detail of the St. Matthew stained glass window (Gerald Tooke, glass artist)

5.16 Mount Allison Chapel, sandstone baptismal font (William McElcheran, sculptor)

When the workmen left to go back to Ontario, Dad went into the chapel and reviewed the windows. He observed that one upper panel, picturing the twelve flames representing the twelve apostles, was upside down.

This time they were able to head off the workmen at the Moncton airport where they were awaiting boarding permission for their flight home. The men returned and looked, and confirmed that [he] was indeed correct. They stayed, removed the portion of the glass panel and corrected the inadvertent error. A good lesson learned was to sometimes stand back and look at the bigger picture as well as focusing on what is up close![17]

Douglas Brown believes "congregations have personalities," and "that personality should be reflected in the form that the building takes."[18] In his eyes, the personality of the Mount Allison Chapel was one of reflection; the space was meant to offer an individual experience.

There were two choices. One was to do a sort of all glass building, which would not have been unusual at that time or for that area, and the other was one that created a certain amount of shelter. We thought of this as being a restful place in a very busy place. So if a student wanted a bit of quiet or a little time, to some extent it was a refuge from the activity and the business of the surrounding campus life ... I think that certainly in my time with the firm, it was probably the best building we did.[19]

At the request of Bruce Brown, who saw it practically as a requirement to have fine art incorporated in his architecture, Canadian artist William McElcheran sculpted the angel and child sandstone font installed near the altar (Figure 5.16). During the late 1950s and the early 1960s, before he established his reputation as a bronze sculptor (his works currently reside in the collection of the National Gallery of Canada), McElcheran worked with Brown, Brisley & Brown as a full-time liturgical artist. McElcheran also designed the chapel furniture, as he worked as a furniture designer in Hamilton before joining the firm.

Officially opened in October of 1965, just a month after the chapel, was the Gairdner Fine Arts Building (Figures 5.18, 5.19). Department head Lawren P. Harris (Figure 5.17) called it "his dream come true"[20] as the Owens had become far too crowded to function effectively as both museum and instruction space. The new

17. Email from C. Jean Cameron to Rhianna Edwards, May 10, 2011.

18. Victoria Drysdale, "Shaping the Way We Worship," in *The Canadian Baptist* (June 1994), p. 25.

19. Douglas Brown interviewed by John Leroux, February 12, 2014.

20. Louis Rombout, "The Changing Phase of the Fine Arts Department," in *Mount Allison Record* (Spring 1966), p. 2. [MAA]

5.17 Fine arts department head Lawren P. Harris standing over a scale model of the Gairdner Fine Arts Building, c.1964

5.18 Gairdner Fine Arts Building (Brown, Brisley & Brown, 1965)

building arrived at a significant point in the history of the fine arts department, as it was in transition from its Magic Realist period—during which such luminaries as Colville, Christopher and Mary Pratt and Tom Forrestall had studied—into a period of deep change. Mount Allison had earned a reputation as one of the leading art schools in Canada, and a new Brown, Brisley & Brown-designed fine arts building further cemented this. Initially considered one of Canada's most modern facilities for teaching art, the Gairdner building soon revealed its limitations. Designed to accommodate a curriculum of painting, graphics and drawing taught by a faculty of only five, the building's initial open plan of a single shared studio on each floor had to be reconfigured as the department grew. Substantial space was required for the introduction of new disciplines, such as photography in the mid-1970s and printmaking in the mid-1980s.

Despite these issues, the building represented a strong expression of faith in the university's fine arts program. Located off the quad between the Owens Art Gallery and the future library, the architects intended the Gairdner building to be evocative of interior (i.e., working) light; they wanted people to look at the building and think 'studios'. To achieve this, they capped the building with a clever blend of a traditional mansard-roof with fully glazed north-facing studio walls. This long break in the copper roof animated the building as busy artists could be seen during the day, and at night it glowed like a lighthouse. Below this upper level, a great solid wall of Wallace sandstone shielded the front entry, surrounded by a grid of vertical ribs encasing red Sackville sandstone slabs and plate glass windows. The Gairdner was connected by a tunnel to the Owens, which, by losing its classroom accommodation, reverted to being primarily an art gallery.

By the fall of 1965, the physical transformation was palpable at Mount Allison. In a front page article in *The United Churchman*, President Cragg remarked that "Alumni and visitors now returning to Mount Allison after a few years absence are amazed at what has happened to the campus. And well they might be. Even the changes made in the past three years amount to a transformation—and the end is not yet!"[21]

Reinventing the university's Conservatory of Music building was a heady task, as Fairweather's Victorian mansion of music was a notable member of the university's architectural family, if a cramped and tired one. Demolition of the ornate structure happened in 1969, as painted wooden turrets and walls came tumbling down with

21. L.H. Cragg, "Mount Allison: Today and Tomorrow," in *The United Churchman* (October 27, 1965), p. 1.

5.19 Gairdner Fine Arts Building, interior stair

the help of diesel excavators. Its companion, the venerable Allison Hall (the former ladies' college building), would follow suit in 1971, the oldest building left from the early days of Mount Allison. The new three-level music building was dedicated to Marjorie Young Bell. A bronze bust of her was unveiled in the lobby just prior to the official opening on October 3, 1966, as was a tablet bearing the words: "Designed to stimulate Music Education and enrich the cultural life of the university and the wide community it serves, these splendid facilities give fitting expression to Mrs. Bell's deep interest in music and Mount Allison."

Possessing the most distinctive outline on campus, the three-pronged layout with its sweeping curved walls was designed to fit the contour of the hill behind the building (Figures 5.20, 5.21). The trio of wings were defined with specific uses: a large two-storey rehearsal room below a choral rehearsal in one, the 371-seat concert and recital auditorium in another and classrooms/studios in the last. At the centre sat an open foyer with a hexagonal mezzanine and beautifully machined railings and a large hexagonal skylight above, and a corresponding terrazzo floor below (Figure 5.22). Other amenities included a substantial music library, recording rooms, practice rooms, an organ room, lounges, instrument storage and a semi-circular reception room that bumped out from the southeastern bow of the building, complete with cut glass chandeliers and tall windows overlooking the swan pond. The Conservatory of Music building's curving, branched plan was similar to another recent New Brunswick project: the Université de Moncton's 1965 Rémi Rossignol science building with its four wings bending out from a central core and a large open rotunda in the middle—in its case, holding up a spiral staircase.

The conservatory building's red Sackville sandstone walls were broken by thin double-storey windows with spandrels at the floor levels, and capped by continuous four-feet deep seamed copper at the edge of the flat roof. This continuous treatment around the building was tempered by a thin concrete canopy above the main entrance, as well as by large fibreglass sculptures hanging off the southern exterior wall (Figure 5.23). These four figures representing a quartet were crafted by William McElcheran, and they were his last artistic contribution to the campus. At the opening ceremony, attended by Premier Louis Robichaud and former Lieutenant-Governor J. Leonard O'Brien, Bruce Brown fittingly said that harmony

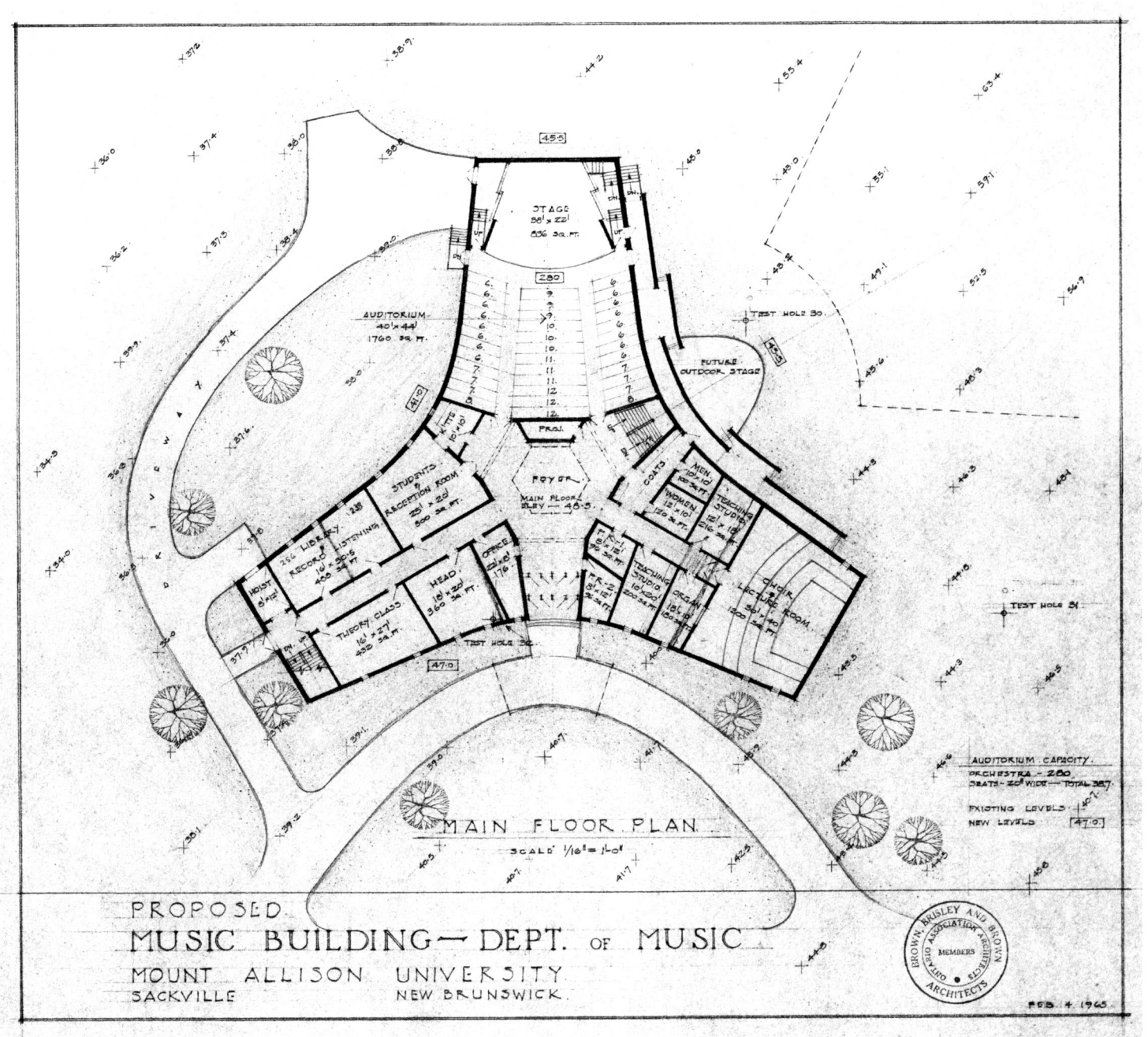

5.20 Marjorie Young Bell Conservatory of Music, schematic ground floor plan and site plan

5.21 Marjorie Young Bell Conservatory of Music (Brown, Brisley & Brown, 1966)

5.22 Marjorie Young Bell Conservatory of Music, central foyer looking up to the hexagonal skylight

"QUARTET FOR OBOE AND STRINGS"

PROPOSED SCULPTURAL TREATMENT FOR
THE MARJORIE YOUNG BELL CONSERVATORY OF MUSIC
MT. ALLISON UNIVERSITY, SACKVILLE N.B.
Wm McELCHERAN, SCULPTOR
SCALE - 3/8" = 1'-0"

5.23 Artist's rendering of the Conservatory of Music building's southern wall showing sculptures of a "quartet for oboe and strings" (William McElcheran, artist & sculptor)

had prevailed throughout the construction period, and he hoped it would continue to prevail inside the building.

Before the Brown, Brisley & Brown period of influence on the campus was underway, it was determined that the cost of repairing and fireproofing Fawcett Hall could not be justified; greater seating capacity was also desired. Fawcett Hall was a fine building with a great deal of character and architectural value, located on a site steeped in Mount Allison history (Charles Allison's home once occupied part of the site), but these factors simply could not compete with the sweeping desire for change. At Mount Allison, as elsewhere at that time, the influence of Modernism was rarely questioned; the cultural value of aged built landscape was seldom considered. In the rush to modernize, Mount Allison was not about to leave Fawcett Hall as a reminder of its whitewashed, wood framed architectural beginnings.

So in October 1966, a striking building was completed along York Street right below the campus hill. The architect was FENCO, which had been awarded the contract before the Brown, Brisley & Brown period began. The building was named the Marjorie Young Bell Convocation Hall (Figure), an imposing brick and stone cube that was a direct descendant of both Fawcett Hall, which it replaced, and the earlier Lingley Hall. A huge mass of a building, it contained a large auditorium and generous lobby set behind a Classical facade of six enormous round columns with an entablature above (Figure 5.25).

FENCO's exterior efforts at blending the old with the new worked well, though the building was clearly of its time with its bronzed aluminum glazing and doors, brown Glasgow brick sides, Modern mansard copper roof cap and relatively clean stone lines (save for the turned Wallace sandstone columns and richly profiled entablature). Great care was taken that the frontal approach embrace the monumental—through the grand stone facade, polished granite steps, terraced stone walkways and the sheer scale of the portico. While it was unquestionably a late-twentieth-century auditorium, it also approvingly referenced the Classical temples of antiquity.

The *Mount Allison Record* relayed the richness of feeling evoked throughout the interior lobby (Figure 5.26):

5.24 Marjorie Young Bell Convocation Hall (FENCO, 1966)

5.25 Marjorie Young Bell Convocation Hall, detail of exterior stone column

5.26 Marjorie Young Bell Convocation Hall, interior lobby

5.27 Marjorie Young Bell Convocation Hall, interior of auditorium showing the seating and upper balcony

5.28 The chemistry building, now called the Barclay Chemistry Building (Brown, Brisley & Brown, 1967)

On entering the building, one is impressed by the spacious three-storied lobby, with its open well extending upward beyond the mezzanine floor to the blue domed ceiling above the balcony level. On either side of the lobby are large cloakrooms and ticket offices. The main lobby walls are faced with beautifully matched Italian figured marble and the entire entrance is attractively lighted by especially designed satin finished gold and cut glass chandeliers and wall brackets.[22]

22. "The Convocation Hall: To Serve a Wide Community," in *Mount Allison Record* (December 1966), p. 5. [MAA]

Do not let this quotation fool you; the enormous chandeliers are Neo-Baroque excess *par excellence*. They are so skillfully executed that they work in the space, anticipating the design indulgence just around the corner in the early 1970s. Beyond the lobby is a 1500-seat carpeted theatre featuring, as well as the lighting and sound equipment, an orchestra pit and one of the largest Casavant organs in eastern Canada (Figure 5.27). The gold curtained stage accommodates recitals, concerts, plays, graduations, addresses, films and more. A large rehearsal room sits below the stage. Other amenities include a green room, dressing rooms, storage and prop rooms, an office and a workshop. While the lack of space in the wings of the stage makes the handling of certain types of performances difficult, overall, Convocation Hall performs its cultural and public duties well. On a sunny day after a convocation ceremony, when the steps and surrounding pathways are packed with well-dressed graduates and their proud families, one might argue that there was no place more splendid in the Maritimes than in front of this hall.

Planning for a new chemistry building was a more complicated process. Brown, Brisley & Brown was in charge of the exterior design, general interior layout and site planning, while the Halifax architecture firm Duffus, Romans, Single and Kundzins looked after the working drawings and supervised the construction. Considered at its outset to be a tremendous facility for teaching undergraduate chemistry, access was through a one-storey glazed entrance pavillion facing the quad. A squared volume with a repeating grid of punched windows along the entire exterior, the chemistry building's skin was set in alternating horizontal runs of red sandstone and cream-coloured stucco (Figure 5.28). Its 50,000 square-feet area possessed seminar rooms, offices, a chemistry library, glass blowing room, student lounge, nine teaching labs, seven research labs and four smaller faculty research labs. This allowed the greatly overcrowded Flemington Science Building next door to get some long-awaited breathing room as a dedicated biology facility.

5.29 Thornton House (left) and Edwards House (right), senior student residences (Brown, Brisley & Brown, 1969)

5.30 Thornton House / Edwards House, interior of a typical dorm room, 1969

Opened in September 1967, Canada's centennial year, Douglas Brown felt that the new chemistry building (later named the Barclay Chemistry Building) was the least interesting of all the buildings his firm designed facing the central quad. These sensibilities may have been driven from above as he thought President Cragg (a chemist) "held back" on that particular building. Cragg encouraged it to be more modest as "he was terribly afraid that he'd be accused of favouring that building … doing something special with the chemistry building that he didn't do for other buildings."[23] This was disappointing as it is the most businesslike of all the central campus buildings. This might have been somewhat countered by a sculpturally-shaped 200-seat lecture theatre that was supposed to push out from the building's face, but the theatre was never built.

Enrollment of baby boomers continued to create a demand for student housing. In October 1969, the university opened two new senior student residences, Thornton House and Edwards House (Figure 5.29, 5.30). This nearly identical pair of L-shaped buildings on Salem Street didn't do much to push design limits; beyond their ashlar sandstone exteriors and inner courtyard, they were fairly mundane residences built to house around 100 students each. With late 1960s mansard roofs (a far cry from their nineteenth-century crafted ancestors) and frugal double-loaded corridor layouts, these buildings suggest that Mount Allison was merely responding to a need and little more. By contrast, and all but forgotten in a basement archival drawer, are drawings of Brown, Brisley & Brown's 1967 residence study schemes: a series of six-storey cubes undulating like tic-tac-toe boxes, scattered across the present male residence site with open green space between them, akin to a poor man's *Ville Radieuse* by Le Corbusier (Figure 5.31).

Construction cranes closed the 1960s as the Ralph Pickard Bell Library neared completion, which officially opened in October 1970 (Figure 5.32). Planning began in January 1966 under the impetus of President Cragg establishing a Library Planning Committee. In the *Mount Allison Record* Cragg declared:

A collection of books—well selected, readily available, growing with the growth of knowledge—is essential to a true university. It is safe to say that the better its library and the more effectively it is used, the better and more effective is a university … [The Memorial Library] has its virtues, but we are resolved to make it much better—and as rapidly as we can …

183

23. Douglas Brown interviewed by John Leroux, February 12, 2014.

5.31 Proposed six-storey residence blocks (Brown, Brisley & Brown, 1967)

5.32 Ralph Pickard Bell Library (Brown, Brisley & Brown, 1970)

Why a new library, instead of another addition to our present building? Partly a matter of lack of space on the present site and of the difficulty of designing an addition so that the enlarged library would be efficient and economic. But mainly it's because ideas of what a university library should be and what services it should provide have undergone such radical changes in the past few years. Gone is the concept of the grand baronial entrance hall, of the lofty spacious reading rooms, of the separated limited-access stacks ...

So different is the modern library that few universities or colleges are making additions to buildings that were designed in the old style. On a tour of leading New England colleges last summer I found that Bowdoin and Amherst were abandoning beautiful and imposing library buildings to other uses and were building entirely new libraries in the modern mode. Our sister university, Victoria (the Toronto one) has done this. So has Alberta. This is what Dalhousie is doing. And we are doing it, not just to be in the swim but because it is the wisest thing to do.[24]

24. L.H. Cragg, "Mount Allison to Have New Library," in *Mount Allison Record* (Spring 1966), pp. 8–9. [MAA]

Replacing the university's overcrowded Memorial Library, which could only hold 140,000 volumes, the new 75,000 square-feet $2-million Bell Library was able to hold 400,000 volumes in its five-storeys—the top three being a structurally expressive interior arrangement of exposed concrete columns and roof beams (Figure 5.33). The exterior was half clad in olive sandstone (at the vertical 'ribs' and horizontal belt courses) and half in red sandstone (at the infill sections and rock-faced base level), with horizontal ribbons of anodized aluminum plate glass windows circling it all.

The new library was unlike any in eastern Canada. While it started its conceptual life in early 1966 as a circular building, it ended up a large octagon in plan with an atrium-like open core, where the rows of book stacks run like spokes from the central axis. One would be forgiven in thinking it was a futuristic attempt at reforming library arrangement, but the exact opposite was the case according to Douglas Brown:

This is a very traditional shape for a library. You look at the Bodleian Library at Oxford or some of these, there's this great central space that goes up and it's lined with books the whole way around. It's a form that's been used over and over again for

5.33 Ralph Pickard Bell Library, interior view of the central atrium

libraries over the centuries, so it seemed to me to make sense. We needed something fairly substantial to anchor that corner of the hill.[25]

25. Douglas Brown interviewed by John Leroux, February 12, 2014.

26. *Mount Allison University President's Report* (1962–63), p. 2. [MAA]

In addition to the stack spaces and circulation desk, the library contained special collection/rare book rooms, university archives, an audio centre, reference area, reading area, periodicals and microfilm rooms, a smoking room, staff workrooms, seminar rooms and a small audio/visual viewing theatre. Varied seating was used throughout, such as study carrels under the top two floors' windows, tables and lounge chairs at the main level and other sundry seating in the other areas.

The approach to handling the hill was a challenge to the architects. Previous wooden buildings aligned with the crest of the rise and faced the town, but the Bell Library presented new challenges. Because of its bulk and size, the designers did not want the building to have a 'back'. All of Brown, Brisley & Brown's Mount Allison buildings—especially the chapel—were multidirectional in their plan as they were intended to be viewed from any direction. An additional feature of the Bell Library site is that the building can also 'see' in every direction—its upper floor rooms have outstanding views into the campus and town, as well beyond to Chignecto Bay.

Not all the campus changes were driven by academic pursuits. To the great relief of students in pursuit of some well-earned leisure (and to those simply skipping classes) the old Memorial Library and its Tweedie Annex were transformed by Brown, Brisley & Brown into the new University Student Centre, opened in March 1971, although it had been identified as a serious need by the university president almost a decade earlier:

One of our great needs is a suitable place for students of both sexes to gather socially with each other and with the faculty during the day or evening. We need a University Centre... In any case we need some unifying influence which will draw faculty and students together more often and in a variety of circumstances; we need a place where men and women can relax together and take part in discussions easily, where they can play bridge, table tennis or other games in decent surroundings; we need an environment where it is possible to listen to good recordings, and to be surrounded by good works of art ... we need a few rooms where campus guests can be taken care of properly; we need a place where Alumni, parents, faculty, friends and students can meet graciously in pleasant surroundings.[26]

5.34 University Centre, Hesler Hall (renovated by Brown, Brisley & Brown, 1971)

27. *Mount Allison University President's Report (1970–71)*, p. 5. [MAA]

Through what the 1970–71 President's Report called "an almost magical metamorphosis,"[27] the crowded book stacks and librarians were traded for student offices, meeting rooms, the university bookstore, a coffee shop and a small theatre. The architects extended the front of the building towards Centennial Hall by about 16 feet, keeping the exact same red stone mass but adding a row of thin windows on the main floor and larger plate glass openings at the basement. The main reading room, with its vaulted ceiling, became Hesler Hall (Figure 5.34), a large student lounge that was surely good for those bridge games, but one that could also be converted to a ballroom by moving aside the sofas and tables.

Over the course of the previous decade, Mount Allison's physical assets had increased in dollar value from approximately $3 million to $16 million. Buildings and financial donations were going up everywhere—but so were costs. While the university endowment had grown fourfold from $3 million to $12 million, the annual expenditure per full-time student (exclusive of board and lodging) had increased from $900 to $2300. Growth had a price, but almost everyone saw the architecture as an indisputable investment. The pervasive student revolts, protests and sit-ins that typified most other North American campuses throughout the late 1960s, including the University of New Brunswick and l'Université de Moncton, never quite took hold on the Mount Allison campus. As the student body stayed the course, their university's most radical changes during the Age of Aquarius were expressed in its physical structures rather than socially and philosophically.

All this modernizing on campus made even stately buildings such as the Owens Art Gallery appear outdated, so it too was not spared from modification. Early 1970s renovations designed by Brown, Brisley & Brown with Gustavo Da Roza of Winnipeg (the architect who designed the unconventional Winnipeg Art Gallery that opened to international praise in 1971) completely altered the interior of the Owens, while a new entrance was created at the building's former rear, facing the central quad. A copper- and stone-clad addition was placed on the quad side of the building, with Frank Lloyd Wright influenced horizontal emphasis on the metal panelling (Figure 5.35). The overall proportions and low hip roof of the Owens were not unlike Wright's turn-of-the-century prairie-style homes such as the famed 1910 Robie House.

Inside the Owens, romantic space and detail were trumped by functionalism.

5.35 Architect's rendering of the Owens Art Gallery renovations and addition (Gustavo Da Roza and Brown, Brisley & Brown, 1972)

28. L. Duchemin, "In retrospect," in *Mount Allison Record* (Spring/ Summer 1974), p. 11. [MAA]

A different way of displaying art had superseded the salon-style hangings of the 1890s. Gone was the two-storey sky-lit central atrium with its symmetrical side gallery plan. Also gone (decades earlier) were the large plaster cast statues that formed the basis for Victorian art training. These were replaced by a more purpose-ful, architectural layout of unadorned white cube rooms in an asymmetrical layout. The galleys's art collection had steadily grown over the decades; space was at a premium. A second gallery level was added over the lower floor entry gallery.

An earlier Brown, Brisley & Brown scheme for the renovation to the Owens Art Gallery (before Da Roza was involved) shows a much more formal and haughty plan than what was eventually built, in which the architects played within the rules of symmetry. It proposes a slightly garnished rectilinear addition with two equal galleries on either side of a central entry. Whether this layout was superior to the scheme that was built is debatable, but it certainly would have reduced the architectural weight and prominence of the adjacent chapel only a few steps away.

It was fortunate that Mount Allison took advantage of its opportunity for widespread growth in the 1960s. By the early 1970s increases in student enrollment levelled off, and an economic recession hovered menacingly over the university. The building boom was over and there was time to reflect on all the many changes that had been made to the campus. As retiring head of the English department, Dr. Lloyd Duchemin recalled in 1974:

The campus of 1974, one of the most beautiful in Canada, could hardly have been imagined in 1954, when we were struggling for mere existence ... the transformation in the physical appearance of Mount Allison has almost the aspect of a miracle which could never have been predicted ... nobody knew or believed that it would happen with such speed.[28]

After this unabashedly forward-looking period, the university took a moment to consider the past, purchasing a local landmark, Cranewood, as the President's House in 1975 (Figure 5.36). Located near the corner of Main and York Streets, the circa 1837 manor is a five-bay red sandstone Georgian house built for notable Sackville resident William Crane; it was later the residence of businessman and politician Josiah Wood. One of Sackville's most historic buildings, it was sold by the

5.36 Cranewood, residence of Mount Allison's president from 1975–2013, (c. 1837)

29. *Mount Allison University President's Report (1975–76)*, p. 26. [MAA]

30. *Mount Allison University Newsletter* (November 19, 1976), p. 4.

university in 2013 when the president moved back into a renovated and restored Hammond House.

The final building designed by a Brown for Mount Allison was a substantial building to house the arts department and the University Computing Centre: the Harold Crabtree Building (Figure 5.37, 5.38). Site plans and study models from the late 1960s show outlines of an exact mirror image of the Bell Library planned for the current Crabtree site, but this was never built (Figure 5.39). Construction costs had continued to escalate, causing repeated delays in settling on a final plan. The Annual President's Report of 1975–76 conveyed that:

another year of disappointment passed as funding has not been obtained for the proposed Arts Building and Admin Link to the Library, designed in 1969 ... Costs have escalated to the point that three times the monies originally projected as needed to build the complex are needed today.[29]

By September 1976, the Board of Regents carried a motion to engage in discussions "on the basis of some project in size and cost amounting to one-third to one-half of the original complex."[30] The structure that was eventually built was designed by the new firm called Douglas Brown Architect—the descendant of Brown, Brisley & Brown after F. Bruce Brown's retirement in 1972.

The Harold Crabtree Building opened to students and faculty in May 1980. Containing classrooms, a large auditorium, the University Computing Centre and headquarters for the psychology and language departments, it had essentially the same exterior wall treatment as the library but on a different mass. The 45 degree orientation of the exterior walls was still there, but no longer in a perfect octagon. Unlike the Bell Library which was a clean Euclidean form, the Crabtree Building bent like a hockey stick along the lines of the existing hill. On the Convocation Hall side, it resembled the configuration of the library; on the quad side it elbowed to create a pathway between it and Hart Hall. Crabtree was subservient to the library and needed to relate to its flanking structure, but the need to match the library may have dominated its design a little too much; the interior of Crabtree is somewhat erratic in circulation and arrangement. The two buildings were tied together, both literally and figuratively, with their matching upper belt-course stone bands, stone

5.37 Harold Crabtree Building (Douglas Brown Architect, 1980)

5.38 Harold Crabtree Building, stonework detail at eastern face

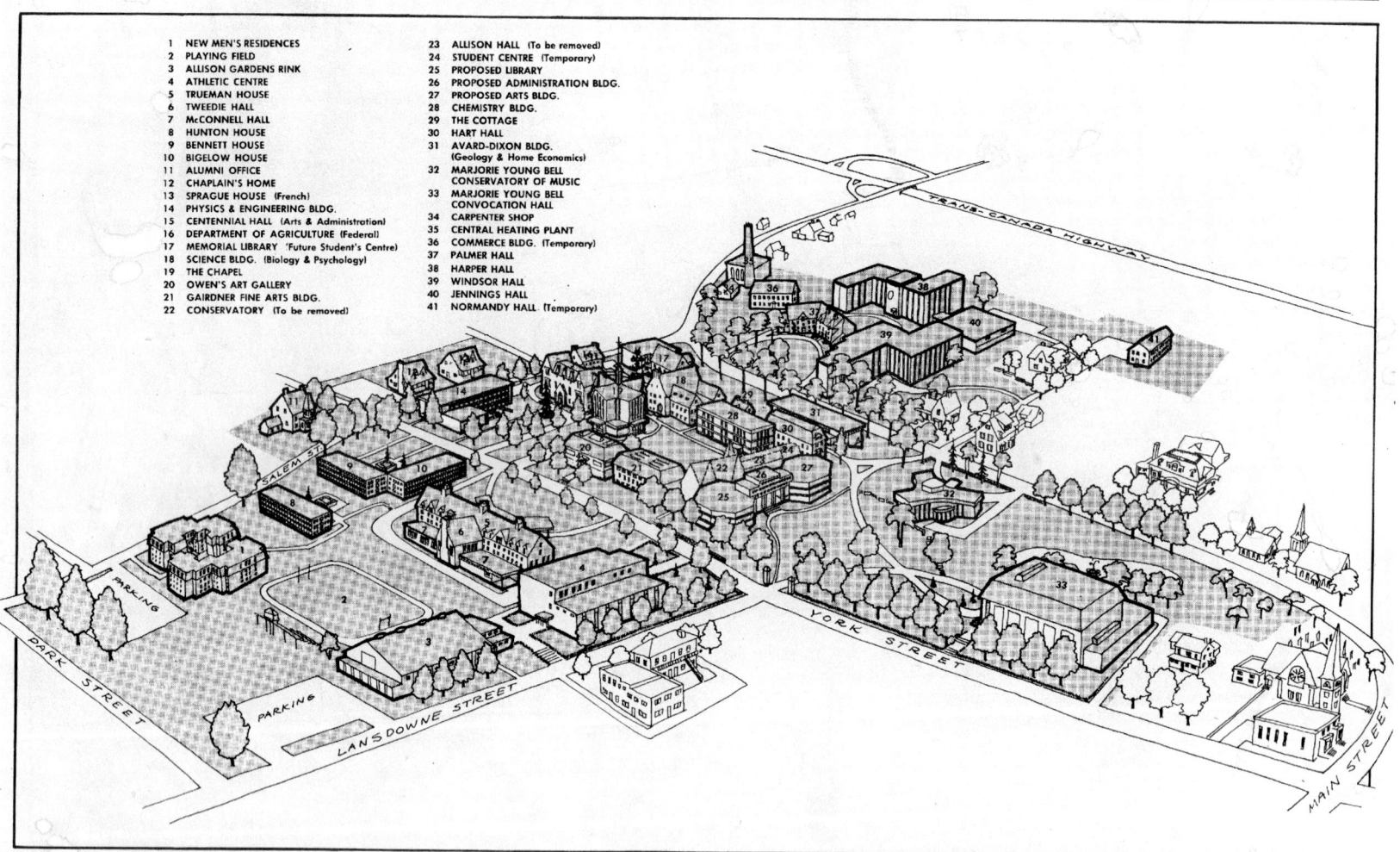

MOUNT ALLISON UNIVERSITY CAMPUS DIRECTORY

SACKVILLE, NEW BRUNSWICK

1 NEW MEN'S RESIDENCES
2 PLAYING FIELD
3 ALLISON GARDENS RINK
4 ATHLETIC CENTRE
5 TRUEMAN HOUSE
6 TWEEDIE HALL
7 McCONNELL HALL
8 HUNTON HOUSE
9 BENNETT HOUSE
10 BIGELOW HOUSE
11 ALUMNI OFFICE
12 CHAPLAIN'S HOME
13 SPRAGUE HOUSE (French)
14 PHYSICS & ENGINEERING BLDG.
15 CENTENNIAL HALL (Arts & Administration)
16 DEPARTMENT OF AGRICULTURE (Federal)
17 MEMORIAL LIBRARY 'Future Student's Centre)
18 SCIENCE BLDG. (Biology & Psychology)
19 THE CHAPEL
20 OWEN'S ART GALLERY
21 GAIRDNER FINE ARTS BLDG.
22 CONSERVATORY (To be removed)

23 ALLISON HALL (To be removed)
24 STUDENT CENTRE (Temporary)
25 PROPOSED LIBRARY
26 PROPOSED ADMINISTRATION BLDG.
27 PROPOSED ARTS BLDG.
28 CHEMISTRY BLDG.
29 THE COTTAGE
30 HART HALL
31 AVARD-DIXON BLDG.
   (Geology & Home Economics)
32 MARJORIE YOUNG BELL
   CONSERVATORY OF MUSIC
33 MARJORIE YOUNG BELL
   CONVOCATION HALL
34 CARPENTER SHOP
35 CENTRAL HEATING PLANT
36 COMMERCE BLDG. (Temporary)
37 PALMER HALL
38 HARPER HALL
39 WINDSOR HALL
40 JENNINGS HALL
41 NORMANDY HALL (Temporary)

5.39 Late 1960s bird's-eye view illustration of Mount Allison showing outlines of the unbuilt mirror of the Bell Library on the current Crabtree site (number 27)

5.40 Late 1960s model of the colonnade with an unbuilt elevated office link between the library and the proposed arts building

5.41 Great colonnade between the library and the Crabtree building

base plinths and an epic element that both enclosed the quad and opened it up to the world.

The most dignified aspect of the Harold Crabtree Building, if not one of the most monumental of all the Brown, Brisley & Brown ideas, was the great colonnade between it and the library (Figure 5.41). The double row of squared sandstone pillars was intended to be the formal opening of the campus to the town of Sackville; a sort of gateway and framed vista. Douglas Brown thought it would be a perfect place to gather and for convocation processions to begin as they meandered down to Convocation Hall. The initial late-1960s design of the colonnade had an elevated link between the two buildings with administration offices (Figure 5.40), but it was abandoned due to cost and impracticality. Instead, the existing colonnade acts mostly as an enhancing element, one that has such venerable precedents as the Brandenburg Gate in Berlin and the peristyle at Michigan's Cranbrook Academy designed by Eliel Saarinen (Figure 5.42).

The opening of the Harold Crabtree Building concluded one of most important architectural adventures in Mount Allison's history. Hiring a firm known almost solely for ecclesiastical architecture was courageous and risky, but the best qualities of the Sackville campus were deeply understood and maintained by Brown, Brisley & Brown. The confident push forward initiated by these architects made the built environment of Mount Allison even more remarkable. The key to Brown, Brisley & Brown's achievement is not only the quality of the individual buildings, but how these buildings were arranged. Set around pedestrian pathways, courtyards and open landscaped surroundings, the rhythmic placement of the campus's sandstone buildings feels so assured that it seems almost inconceivable that it could have ever been otherwise. While the University of Toronto may have more masterpieces, and Arthur Erickson's Simon Fraser mountaintop campus outside Vancouver may have been more influential, Brown, Brisley & Brown's work at Mount Allison should be lauded as one of the most powerful university transformations in Canadian history.

5.42 Cranbrook Academy peristyle, Bloomfield Hills, Michigan (Eliel Saarinen, 1942)

CHAPTER SIX

The Constant of Change
1980–

Mount Allison University saw almost no major building activity during the 1980s. After the massive outburst of energy and funds that framed the building projects of the 1960s and early 1970s, the university found that its needs were adequately met by its current built environment. Stable enrollment through the 1970s combined with the severe economic recessions of the early 1980s and early 1990s created few incentives for embarking on new construction projects, and so no large architectural projects would be undertaken until the new millennium.

When needs arose, they could often be met by purchasing and renovating older off-campus buildings and so most campus construction projects would be medium-sized renovations. Such projects include: the linking of the Hammond studio and barn to create Bermuda House Residence by Moncton's Robert Eaton Architect; Hart Hall's refurbishment; and the recladding of Bennett, Bigelow and Hunton houses by B. Burtt Barteaux & Associates of Halifax.

Other renovations were so extensive that the original buildings were barely recognizable by the time the plywood hoarding was removed and the changes were revealed. Major rebuilds of the Physics and Engineering Building and the Avard-Dixon Building also concealed their Modernist roots and would greatly change the appearance of Mount Allison, shifting buildings away from their original design language and materials. Such changes were part of the profound critique of Modern architecture that was gaining ground in North America, a backlash which was gaining momentum in the Maritimes by the mid to late 1970s. To a great extent, the backlash was provoked by the perception that the Modernist aesthetic, as expressed in architecture and planning, had reneged on its promise to create a better world through design. As a result, a serious disconnect developed between what the general public valued in its built environment and what Modernism appeared to be providing.

While there were many instances of successful design during the Modernist period, negative opinions were widespread and reactionary voices found a sympathetic audience. The worldwide upheaval resulted in a new architectural movement known as Postmodernism—a philosophy that mushroomed during the 1980s as critics questioned the core values of much architecture which followed the Second World War. Postmodernism advocated a return to the signs and symbols of the architectural past and the use of traditional design, materials and construction methods. Sometimes labelled Neotraditionalism, the Postmodern style endeavoured to reestablish architectural empathy and establish a link to bygone building methods and local inspiration.

Postmodernism, however, was no magic pill; it had its own drawbacks. It could be derivative, promoting a shallow application of past architectural forms and materials. To make a building 'contextual' requires much more than the simple use of pointed roofs, imitation ornament or fake window mullions. Like the weaker examples of Modernist buildings that Postmodernism correctly critiqued, it was easy to superficially apply Postmodernism to a building without embracing the essence of the building's purpose or the nature of its site—the starting points for any good design. In retrospect, history will judge whether Postmodernism offered a credible design approach that truly reflected our time, as Alex Colville urged several decades before.

Unfortunately, due to tight budgets and diminished standards, projects undertaken in New Brunswick during the Postmodern craze typically did not go much beyond a superficial pasting-on of ornament and 'cutesifying' buildings. In several cases at Mount Allison, renovations intended to make older structures more palatable instead exposed an institutional disconnection with architectural history and expression, and perhaps even with the narrative of the university's own architectural evolution.

In the case of the Avard-Dixon Building, Sackville architect Arthur J. Arseneau was engaged to design a complete renovation to the structure, both inside and out, and a Postmodern sensibility ruled. Opening in 1994, the $2.7 million project would house the social sciences (geography, commerce, education, sociology/anthropology and economics) and the Meighen Centre for Learning Assistance and Research. A fourth floor that was planned in 1959 but not built was also added (Figure 6.1). The exterior concrete block/glass/panel skin was removed and replaced with the now familiar rock-faced red sandstone in a random ashlar pattern. The ribbon glazing was changed to a spare fenestration of punched square windows with divided lites and stone lintels. A shingled hip roof was placed above the top floor, with wood-clad gabled dormers periodically marching along the edge. The original grey granite entry portal facing Main Street was maintained, along with its colourful abstract ceramic tile mural by Lawren P. Harris (Figure 4.16)—albeit just barely. Lamentably, the significance of the exterior artwork was not brought to the attention of the contractors during the renovation. It would have been destroyed by hammers in minutes had it not been for Virgil Hammock, former head of the fine arts department, who was alerted by a passerby that workers were starting to shatter off the tiles. Hammock ran over, "essentially put my body between the workers and the mural,"[1] and alerted the administration to the skirmish. The administration gave instructions to preserve the mural.

There is nothing inherently unpleasant about the remodelled Avard-Dixon Building—its use of the red sandstone is well executed, as are the overall detailing and massing, and it is certainly approachable. But its attempt to recreate a sense of a 'traditional' Mount Allison building is tentative. What was the affront of the original building? The flat roof? Ribbon windows? Composite panels and concrete block? Whether the administration disliked these Modernist traits, or whether the allure of red sandstone uniformity was too strong to resist, the adventurous technical and social spirit of an important Mount Allison building was misunderstood and the forces of nostalgia and sentimentality altered it a point of predictability. While the Avard-Dixon Building's new stone skin may have appeared to better align with the visual language of the campus's brand, a pluralistic mix of styles and materials would have been much more in keeping with the architectural narrative of Mount Allison.

Admittedly, the wave of architectural romanticism was also influencing other Maritime universities, such as St. Francis Xavier and Acadia. Unlike Dalhousie's campus, which was shaped by an urban setting in downtown Halifax and an allied architecture school, the small town campuses in Antigonish and Wolfville have recently pursued a neotraditional Georgian image that projects a somewhat edited version of the Maritimes' architectural past. This shift in image is rooted in safer,

1. Virgil Hammock interviewed by John Leroux, August 2014.

6.1 Avard-Dixon Building (renovated by Arthur J. Arseneau Architect, 1994)

2. Steven Mannell, "The Dream (and Lie) of Progress: Modern Heritage, Regionalism, and Folk Traditions in Atlantic Canada," in *Journal of the Society for the Study of Architecture in Canada* (2011, vol. 36, no. 1), pp. 102–103.

3. *Campus Notebook* (March/April 2000), p. 4. [MAA]

more homogenized assumptions about what a contemporary east-coast campus should look like, assumptions that cater more to tourism than to the actual historical record. As architectural historian Steven Mannell explains in his essay *The Dream (and Lie) of Progress*, the reverse ought to be championed:

So why worry about modern heritage in a region where many feel that modernity has failed? There are the worthy reasons, including our obligation to bear witness to the continuum of our heritage, not just to an imagined once-upon-a-time 'golden age' ... Our built modern heritage is a legacy of ambition, will and symbolism, left for our benefit and use by those who came before us; it is folly to ignore the significant embodied energy, both cultural and material, in modern buildings. It is puzzling that contemporary Atlantic Canadians are easily motivated to conserve buildings from the premodern era, a time that most would find oppressive to inhabit in social, political and economic terms, yet are uncomfortable recognizing the value of the built heritage of the post-war era, which expresses such legacies as democratization, human rights, social mobility, access to education and health care, access to decent housing and the arts, women's and minority rights, and improved standards of living. [2]

Several years later, Mount Allison's Physics and Engineering Building would suffer the same fate, transforming in 2000 into the stone-clad Sir James Dunn Building, housing the computer science, math and physics departments. Architecture 2000 Inc. of Moncton designed the substantial 'renovation'—although it was essentially a full rebuild, right down to the bare structural skeleton. The new facility gained accessibility, greater energy efficiency, the addition of an experiential mode physics lab, a videography room, new computer labs, improved teaching and research space and a new fourth floor under a dormered hip roof. But it also lost something by playing it safe. As an April 2000 article admitted, the new sandstone exterior finish gave the building "a similar look to other buildings on campus"[3] (Figure 6.2). While the original Physics and Engineering Building may not have been considered a significant campus landmark, it reflected an important time in the development of the campus as well as scientific and technical advancement in New Brunswick. It was altered shortly before mid-century Modernism began to be appreciated again. The 1958 Physics and Engineering Building was distinctive

6.2 Sir James Dunn Building (renovated by Architecture 2000 Inc., 2000)

6.3 Jennings Dining Hall (renovated by A+ Design, 1999)

and openly communicated its teaching role through its architectural envelope and bare materials. By contrast, the Sir James Dunn Building's form could just as easily house a student residence, a fact easily grasped by comparing it to nearby Campbell Hall.

Other renovations around the turn of the century included the refurbishment of Jennings, Windsor and Harper halls (now co-ed residences), the new landscaped quad between them, and a large glass greenhouse that filled the gap between the biology and chemistry buildings.

In 1999, Jennings Dining Hall was substantially renovated by A+ Design of Moncton, the forerunner to Architecture 2000 (Figures 6.3, 6.4). Jennings took over as the main residence dining hall for the campus, as the McConnell dining halls were closed and their patrons shifted over to the once female-only hall. As well as gaining wheelchair accessibility, the new facility's functional layout was changed to a market-style service and a more prominent and welcoming entry rotunda was added facing the quadrangle. A similar rotunda and other improvements would soon touch up the adjacent Harper Hall. Permanent outdoor tables and chairs would also be placed in the sunken courtyard between Jennings and Windsor halls.

In 2004, Harper Hall saw its unappealing entry—a 1960s four-storey solid brick wall with a small cavity entry at the bottom corner—changed for the better. Halifax's Sperry & Partners designed a more hospitable four-storey rotunda that used matching brick and faceted windows to create lounges at each floor and give a more appropriate sheltered entry portal (Figure 6.5). New finishes and furnishings also refreshed the interior. Shelf angle repairs behind the exterior brick surface necessitated new masonry bands at each floor level, so grey brick strips soon wrapped around the perimeter of both Harper and Windsor halls.

But as brick was going up, stone would soon come down. Palmer Hall was the oldest student residence on campus, a gorgeous and alluring building that evoked historic Sackville through its red sandstone and carved details. Regrettably, it appeared far sturdier than it actually was. By the early 1990s the entire rear wall was failing, so it was rebuilt stone by stone with each being numbered, catalogued and carefully removed for the repair (see frontispiece, page 2). All stones were put back in their original place when the job was completed. Regrettably, by the early 2000s water infiltration and pressure from the roots of the tall pine tree in its front yard had shifted the house's foundation, contributing to Palmer Hall's ultimate

6.4 Jennings Dining Hall, interior view

6.5 Harper Hall (renovated by Sperry & Partners architects, 2004)

6.6 Campbell Hall (Sperry & Partners architects, 2004)

6.7 View looking into the north residence quad (left to right: Campbell Hall, Harper Hall, Windsor Hall) with the Avard-Dixon Building in the foreground

6.8 Wallace McCain Student Centre (Renovated by Sperry & Partners architects, 2008)

demise. The prospect of retaining the house's facade was explored but deemed unfeasible. Contemporary building code and accessibility requirements were the final straw. Palmer Hall was demolished in 2003.

A new co-ed residence named Campbell Hall was designed for the hallowed site (which had also been the location of the first three Mount Allison academy buildings) by Sperry & Partners architects, Mount Allison's go-to architects of the period. The design for the new residence was initially intended to mirror the aesthetics of nearby Harper Hall, but instead took a different path. Framing the residence quad was key, and the new building footprint had a similar bow to Palmer Hall, but was now faced inwards towards Harper, Jennings and Windsor halls. This was understandable, but its indifference to the street which it turns its back to is unfortunate. Initial renderings of the scheme showed a flat-roofed four-storey building with a central cylindrical entrance and lounge bump, but in the end the design deferred somewhat to the demolished Palmer Hall with its pitched roof, undulating bays, gabled dormers with paired windows and the obligatory red sandstone cladding with olive stone framing around the windows and openings (Figures 6.6, 6.7). The Harper-esque cylinder rotunda idea was kept, but faceted to make it appear less Modern.

Fully accessible with single rooms and semi-private washrooms, Campbell Hall effectively doubled the capacity of its predecessor, housing 162 students. Opened in the fall of 2004, Campbell Hall's use of sustainable technologies such as extensive insulation, heat-recovery ventilation, water conserving washroom fixtures and smart lighting not only helped to save the university on annual energy costs, it also won a national energy efficiency award in 2005. The new structure was comfortable and popular, but its architecture projected a definite aura of historicism—a safe choice that stayed clear of any genuine attempt at architectural innovation.

One of the most significant building transformations of the early twenty-first century at Mount Allison was the renovation of Trueman House. In the 1990s, campus residences were slowly beginning to convert to co-ed arrangements. When the decision was taken to make Trueman co-ed in the fall of 1994, a group of residents opposed the incursion of females so vehemently, they actually camped out on the lawn for several days in sub-zero temperatures in protest. They were on the wrong side of social change, but the eventual co-ed residence lasted only a decade. In the mid-2000s the residence was closed and Sperry & Partners were

4. Robert Eaton Architect Limited, *The Sustainable University Campus: Guidelines for Environmentally-Responsible Campus Planning. Mount Allison University: Sackville, New Brunswick* (1994), p. 3.

hired to convert Trueman House into a shiny new multi-purpose student centre with a restored exterior. Major architectural changes included new windows, the removal of the awkward mid-1960s concrete canopy over the front entrance and the creation of lounges surrounding the new sky-lit atrium that opened right through every level of the building. Reopened in September 2008 as the Wallace McCain Student Centre (Figure 6.8), the rejuvenated structure united many previously scattered services under one roof. These included the registrar and admissions office, the campus bookstore, the Meighen Centre, the student health centre, fitness and wellness centres, student organization offices, campus pub and café, cafeteria, meeting rooms, headquarters for the student radio station and newspaper, an international student centre, a multi-faith prayer room and even a coin-operated laundry facility.

By the early 1990s, Mount Allison lacked a comprehensive campus plan or official policy for dealing with its grounds and buildings. In 1994, Sackville architect Robert Eaton compiled a National-Research-Council-funded analysis of the university that articulated what he saw as problems and potentials. Using other universities' master plans as case studies, Eaton's report employed similar strategies for mapping Mount Allison's environmentally significant areas, open spaces, buildings and circulation patterns. It pushed for an environmentally responsible campus that exhibited "a greater awareness of the ecological, historical and built context,"[4] and encouraged the administration to create a formal master plan that would help guide its future development for the next 20 years.

Following this concept, Mount Allison engaged the renowned Canadian firm Diamond and Schmitt Architects to prepare a 20-year Facilities Master Plan. Approved in principle by the Board of Regents in 2002, the extensive, campus-wide plan was an evolving blueprint intended to guide the university on how best to adapt to the changing needs of its facilities, academic programs and students. The plan was to centre the campus around three primary areas: a residential area, a consolidated academic area and a centralized student area. Highlights (some of which have been acted upon) included:

* Construction of a new residence to replace the ailing Palmer Hall, and consolidating the meal-plan residences on the north side of campus, near Jennings Dining Hall;

* Centralization of student activities in a renovated Trueman/McConnell Hall;
* Consolidation of the fine arts department and the drama program in a new building within the central campus;
* Renovation and expansion of the Athletic Centre and Hart Hall;
* Design and construction of new residences at the periphery of the campus, replacing the older men's residences along Salem Street;
* Renovation of the Gairdner Fine Arts Building into the University Archives;
* Reinforce existing and potential quadrangles with additions and new building sites to define outdoor rooms; and
* Renovation of satellite houses owned by Mount Allison.

The most notable of the "satellite houses" referred to above was Colville House, a circa 1879 residence on York Street that was the home of Alex Colville from 1949 to 1973 (Figure 6.9). This was a seminal period in his growth as an artist, making it somewhat of a shrine to Canadian visual art. In a 1982 interview, Colville recalled:

In May of '49 we bought that house ... for $5,000. It was in very bad physical condition. I mention this because it had a very important effect on me as an artist, and even as a teacher in a way ... George Slipp (a veteran and third year fine arts student) and I did all the carpenter work, the roofing, the digging, the reglazing, interior woodwork and everything, and that was a very interesting experience for me because I got into the actual business of construction and the whole idea of measuring. I had made scale drawings of the house plans and elevations and all that initially.... And in the spring of 1950 I did my first, as I guess I have often said to people, my first good painting which was called Nude and Dummy. *I am sure [it] was a kind of direct product of the mural that I had done in '48 and of the house building and constructive stuff that I had done in '49, because it was an interior scene—in fact an actual room in that house, a bedroom.*[5]

Nude and Dummy is a personal and reflective depiction of Colville's wife Rhoda set in the house's attic. Along with *Horse and Train* (1954), which was also painted here, it is considered one of his first significant canvases. The building was purchased by Mount Allison in 1981 and initially served as a student residence.

5. Alex Colville interviewed by John Reid, January 20, 1982. [MAA, 8253]

6.9 Colville House, former home of Alex Colville from 1949 to 1973 (c.1879)

In 2009 it was transformed into Colville House, an interpretive centre honouring Mount Allison's celebrated alumnus.

An atypical architectural project, but noteworthy as a unique design on the campus, was the Gemini Observatory, built in 2008 at the corner of York and Salem Streets. A solar-powered astronomical facility containing two 3.5-metre diameter domes with electric rotation capability and shutters, the observatory proudly housed a pair of Celestron 11-inch Schmidt-Cassegrain telescopes. A groundswell of a project, it was built over the summer and assembled entirely by a group of volunteers made up of Mount Allison students, staff and faculty.

As the second decade of the millennium opened, the Gemini Observatory was not the only spot on campus where people were looking skyward. It was no secret that the fine arts department had long been constrained for space in the Gairdner Building. The growing department had resorted to occupying various spaces in other campus buildings, but this was not a suitable long-term arrangement. As discussions with the administration unfolded, a plan to assemble the various fine arts disciplines together under one roof gained support and was soon extended to include the addition of a new theatre for the performing arts (as per the 2002 Master Plan). It was time for an ambitious new vision, for the construction of a new facility which would be architecturally and spiritually uplifting—a twenty-first century sanctuary where space and light could inspire creativity and collaboration.

One of Canada's foremost architecture firms, Zeidler Partnership Architects of Toronto, were engaged to design what would become the Purdy Crawford Centre for the Arts, a stunning work of contemporary architecture which establishes the initial view of Mount Allison when approaching the campus by Main Street from the highway. The roots of the Zeidler firm go back to 1880 when architect William Blackwell established his practice in Peterborough, Ontario. Critical to the firm's development was emigration of Bauhaus-trained architect Eberhard Zeidler from Germany in 1951. Zeidler joined the firm and became a partner in 1955, eventually moving the company to Toronto in the early 1960s and renaming it Craig, Zeidler and Strong in 1963. Over the past five decades Zeidler Partnership has produced some of the most praised buildings in Canada, including Ontario Place in Toronto (1971), the McMaster University Health Sciences Centre (1972), the Toronto Eaton Centre (1977), Canada Place at Vancouver's Expo 86 (1986), the Mississauga Living Arts Centre (1998) and the Bow skyscraper in Calgary (2012, in partnership

6.10 Purdy Crawford Centre for the Arts (Zeidler Partnership Architects, 2014)

6.11 Purdy Crawford Centre for the Arts, Motyer-Fancy Theatre

with Foster + Partners of London). An internationally-recognized design firm, Zeidler has satellite offices in Calgary, Victoria, Beijing, Shanghai and Chengdu (China), Abu Dhabi, Berlin, and London. Architects of this consequence rarely undertake projects in New Brunswick, so Zeidler's involvement on the Mount Allison campus represented an extraordinary opportunity for the region.

Opened in the fall of 2014, the Purdy Crawford Centre for the Arts is arguably the finest university facility in Canada for the teaching of fine and performing arts, and one of the foremost instances of contemporary design in eastern Canada. Designed by senior Zeidler partner Tarek El-Khatib, the 50,000 square-feet facility is distinguished by its contemporary form—a conspicuous break from nearby structures. Unrepentant about its hulking exterior mass, its dramatic facades are covered with the traditional Mount Allison arrangement of rock-faced red sand-stone. In a playful contemporary gesture, the large volumes are broken down by long window slices that run vertically and horizontally throughout (Figure 6.10). Embellishing the exterior campus spaces was also key, as the south facade of the building would complete a quadrangle formed by Centennial Hall, the Flemington Science Building and the Bennett Building.

With a strategy centred on linking diverse spaces through a common spine, the Purdy Crawford Centre for the Arts building is fundamentally a set of three interconnected buildings that enclose entry courtyards and a dynamic interior hall, creating what El-Khatib calls "a village for the arts."[6] The southern long wing houses two levels of lofty studio spaces and workshops, the northwest wing contains a 100-seat flexible theatre with retractable seating (Figure 6.11), while the thin northeast wing has offices on the ground floor, photo studios and darkrooms above, and open studios on the third floor. The multi-level circulation/common area is flooded with natural light, intended to encourage the casual interactions that are often the catalysts to new artistic ideas. The multi-storey atrium lobby frames an impressive exterior view, punctuated by the heating plant building's soaring brick smokestack. The atrium's centrepiece is the floating, twisting black steel stair enclosed by stainless-steel mesh, its structure soaring around the elevator shaft (Figure 6.12). The architects saw the great multi-level connecting hall as "a meeting place for exhibition, experimentation, crits, play, lounge and rehearsal."[7] The design is conceived as the northern gateway to the campus for pedestrians walking from Main Street through to the campus quad, or for the public who come

215

6. Peter Sealy, "Making a Scene," in *Canadian Architect* (March 2015), p. 18.

7. *Mount Allison University Purdy Crawford Centre for the Arts: Sackville, New Brunswick* (2015), p. 2. A promotional brochure produced by Zeidler Partnership Architects, Toronto.

to take in a performance in the theatre. The centre's structural bones are expressed throughout the interior, with steel columns and cross-bracing exposed wherever possible, as well as open-grid ceiling systems. The design also includes energy efficient mechanical and electrical systems, LED lighting, high performance glass walls and sustainable materials. The lighting almost works magic at night as it glitters like sequins through the glass, making the oscillating window pattern come alive.

Evident in the design of this structure is the fact that contemporary Modernism is free from the rules of the past. Where Mies van der Rohe's geometrical severity could not tolerate a non-repeating window grid or uninterrupted lines of glass (as the original Physics and Engineering Building or the Avard-Dixon building attested), the flexibility and playfulness of the rhythmic use of windows in the Purdy Crawford Centre is a reflection of the design placing windows exactly where they need to be, rather than allowing previous iterations of form to impose their location. This is revealed by instances such as the studios' and workshops' clerestory strip windows, which bathe the student areas with working light.

When a structure is expressly dedicated to the pursuit of art, one desires to encounter the unexpected in its design and construction, for the rules to be broken and for a playfulness to be expressed that belies the technical seriousness of the exercise. The Purdy Crawford Centre delivers. Enhancing the lightness of the glazing, the building's stone mass hits you at first glance and yet is transformed into an energetic play of structural buoyancy and lift. Not all of the exterior stone walls run to the ground; they are mostly set above horizontal bands of glazing and panels at the ground floor. In addition, some cantilevered walls hover past their bearing points, underscoring the actual lightness of contemporary construction. The rhythm established by the openings and the building edges, all outlined with dark metal frames, highlights the rich texture of the sandstone. This is further enhanced by courtyard walls that run inward at the north and eastern ends, clad in large white fibre-cement panels, the variation of texture and colour conveying a sense of lightness.

Just as the placement and architectural expression of the Mount Allison Chapel embodied the university's wider transformation of the 1960s, so too might the Purdy Crawford Centre herald a new direction for the campus at the beginning of the twenty-first century. Both structures speak to the boldness of a particular

6.12 Purdy Crawford Centre for the Arts, interior atrium staircase wrapping around the elevator shaft

moment in time and to a clarity of vision that inspired the university to move beyond the expected and to build structures that were much more than mere bricks and mortar fulfilling a function. Both projects demonstrated faith in the future and an understanding of the role exalted architecture can play in spurring us to enlightenment. While the chapel is compact and vertical in its thrust as the epicentre of the campus, the Purdy Crawford Centre is sweeping and horizontal, a kindred spirit to the vast openness of the nearby marshes. While the gestures may be different, elemental to the success of both the Mount Allison Chapel and the Purdy Crawford Centre for the Arts are ingredients too rarely seen in today's restrained building climate: quality and integrity.

Although the design of the Purdy Crawford Centre for the Arts was praised and welcomed by many, its reception was not universally positive. Some felt the stone mass at the corner of Main and Salem streets was too blunt an introduction to the campus, and the retaining walls at the corner are indeed heavy-handed and clunky. A more significant objection was that the construction required the demolition of Andrew Cobb's 1927 Memorial Library and C.A. Fowler's 1960 Tweedie Annex—both significant buildings with historical and architectural worth. Early in the planning process, several options were explored that incorporated the Memorial Library, but the cost of pursuing these options was seen as prohibitive. The university administration felt that a stand-alone scheme allowed for a project that used the site more efficiently, and it decided against saving the older structures. On campus and off, people stepped forward to advocate for the preservation of the 1927 section. The "Save the Memorial Library" campaign went as far as lobbying the provincial government's Minister of Wellness, Culture and Sport to protect the building, but ultimately these efforts were unsuccessful. It is perhaps not surprising that none of the public outcry advocated for the importance of the adjoining Tweedie Annex, a Modernist structure which was maligned and underappreciated later in its life. It was characterized as a sacrificial lamb that could be let go as long as Memorial Library was saved, demonstrating a lack of public understanding of the significance of this structure and of the broader value of mid-century Modern architecture in the Maritimes.

Despite the advantages gained with the construction of this new building and

its dramatic visual impact, the transformative nature of the Purdy Crawford
Centre for the Arts may take time to gain more universal appreciation, but such is the nature of architectural reform. The Transamerica Pyramid in San Francisco was scorned when it first towered over the city in the early 1970s, yet over time it has become one of the great symbols of the city and a much admired landmark. Change is sometimes hard to accept, but a broader appreciation of the arc of Mount Allison's architectural history may foster a more tempered perspective.

We may now be in the middle of one of the greatest periods of campus architecture in Canadian History. The Perimeter Institute for Theoretical Physics (University of Waterloo), Schulich School of Music (McGill University), Leslie Dan Pharmacy Building and the Scarborough Academic Resource Centre (University of Toronto), Schulich School of Business (York University) and, closer to home, the University of New Brunswick's Hans W. Klohn Commons, all point to a renewed wave of construction bringing a new generation of humanistic and confident structures to our university campuses, fostering rich spaces of light, material and flow. The Purdy Crawford Centre for the Arts is Mount Allison's contribution to this contemporary burst of great buildings. This bodes well for the students of today and those who will soon follow. While architecture may not change the world in its own right, our best structures certainly create an environment that might nurture the initiatives and ideas that will.

Conclusion

Over 175 years, the constant at Mount Allison has been change in the physical environment. A recurring renewal of campus buildings and outdoor spaces is one of the most powerful elements in the institution's evolution. It is by no means an excuse to discount the remaining heritage structures or the exceptional qualities of Mount Allison's idyllic campus environment, but it is useful to keep in mind that every building currently standing on the campus was a replacement for one that stood before. These buildings—both the present ones and the ones that live in memory—were each and every one contemporary for their time and designed with the purpose of helping youthful minds grow, educating the next generation of citizens. There is deep resonance in the pluralism that guided Mount Allison in becoming one of the most beautiful and cherished campuses in Canada. The sense of pride that students, alumni, faculty, staff and the wider community have for this place and its assembly of architecture is one of the strongest ties that binds them together. It is a lesson that should be heeded as we continue building and rebuilding this little corner of the world.

What would Charles Allison think of his namesake university 175 years after his bold proposition in 1839 to establish a school for boys? Setting aside the vast social and technological changes that would have seemed inconceivable to Allison and his colleagues, how could he not be delighted? Mount Allison's family of buildings continue to promote excellence in students and teachers. Ultimately, they exist to instill in all those who pass through their halls a desire to live inspired lives of integrity, engagement and purpose. The architecture has been an essential part of the journey; it has led by example, sometimes quietly, sometimes forcefully.

New Brunswick has not had an easy time over the last century when it comes to its architectural record. While there are a few exceptions, we have not always pulled our weight when it comes to the design and construction of great buildings. There are a handful of truly transcendent university buildings throughout Canada,

1. Winston Churchill in a speech to the House of Commons, October 28, 1943. The parliament was meeting in the House of Lords.

including Massey College at the University of Toronto and the Museum of Anthropology at the University of British Columbia. Although seldom acknowledged, one such exemplar sits at the centre of Mount Allison's campus: the Mount Allison Chapel. While it is hardly ever spoken of in those terms, it deserves to be. It is possibly the finest building erected in New Brunswick in the past century.

And why does this matter? Is it not enough to suggest that such an architectural jewel was built in Sackville due merely to the convergence of an expanding campus, architectural talent and the availability of funding? No, there is more to it than that. This achievement was the result of Mount Allison's century-long legacy of crafting structures that had meaning and purpose in equal measure. If a place matters, and the task you undertake in that place matters, then the buildings should matter. This university matters, and it matters a lot. You can feel it when you arrive at the edge of the campus and encounter its stone-clad structures guarding their position; and you can feel it even more as you walk through the campus—which is the way it was designed to be experienced. The architectural presence seems consistent at first, but it soon expands to a harmony of buildings and landscaped spaces. Idiosyncrasies emerge as vistas open and shift, transforming the masses of stone, brick and glass into dynamic presences invigorating the space around them. This is a destination that takes on meaningfulness, a place where human hands seem to have given magic and charisma tangible form. It is that rarest of situations where you feel comfortable and energized at the same time; a place where impact and serenity coexist.

Yet the slow and measured evolution of Mount Allison was not inevitable. On so many levels and at so many stages during its lifetime, this institution could have gone off the rails due to any number of challenges or economic roadblocks. Fortunately, rational and informed heads prevailed, and these buildings embody those institutional and community values. Architects, contractors, labourers, artists, donors, faculty, administrators, students, maintenance staff, townspeople and politicians—each have played their part in the making of Mount Allison.

Is it too much to expect a textured stone wall or a pleasant walkway to change someone's outlook? Do rigorous design and well-constructed execution furnish a building with means to do more than shelter and surround? The values embodied in our best buildings certainly do. Winston Churchill articulated that "we shape our buildings and afterwards our buildings shape us."[1] At Mount Allison University,

View from the north residence quad to the main campus: (left to right) Windsor Hall, Avard-Dixon Building, Barclay Chemistry Building, President's Cottage, Campbell Hall

224   the shaping (and perpetual reshaping) of the built environment within the wider landscape has been one of its greatest achievements, affecting thousands upon thousands of individuals over nearly two centuries. Often taken for granted, the architecture of Mount Allison should not be considered lightly. It makes you want to be here, to revel in the pleasure of learning in this exceptional place. It motivates us to care about this university, this town, this province, this country, to care about honouring the sacrifices and vision of those that came before, and to care about the legacy we will leave for those who are yet to come. In many ways it exemplifies something more profound: a way forward, the best we can be.

Official Names used by the Institution

A. MALE ACADEMY

Mount Allison Wesleyan Academy (1843–53)

Mount Allison Wesleyan Academy, Male Branch (1854–68)

Mount Allison Wesleyan Male Academy (1869–79)

Mount Allison Wesleyan Academy (1880–88)

Mount Allison Academy (1889–1936)

Mount Allison Academy and Commercial College (1936–53)

Closed in 1953

B. FEMALE ACADEMY / LADIES' COLLEGE

Mount Allison Wesleyan Academy, Female Branch (1854–68)

Mount Allison Wesleyan Female Academy (1869–76)

Mount Allison Wesleyan Ladies' Academy (1877–86)

Mount Allison Wesleyan Ladies' College (1887–93)

Mount Allison Ladies' College (1894–1936)

Mount Allison School for Girls (1936–46)

Closed in 1946

C. COMMERCIAL COLLEGE

Mount Allison Commercial College (1874–1936)

Mount Allison Academy and Commercial College (1936–53)

Mount Allison Commercial College/School (1953–55)

Closed in 1955

D. MOUNT ALLISON COLLEGE / UNIVERSITY

Mount Allison Wesleyan College (1862–85)

University of Mount Allison College (1886–1913)

Mount Allison University (1913–present)

Mount Allison's Architects and their Buildings

A+ DESIGN

Jennings Dining Hall (renovation, 1999)

GORDON ADAMSON AND ASSOCIATES

Windsor Hall (1963)

Harper Hall (1965)

Jennings Hall (1965)

ALWARD & GILLIES

Science building [Flemington Science Building] (co-designers, 1931)

ARCHITECTURE 2000

Sir James Dunn Building (renovation, 2000)

ARTHUR J. ARSENEAU

Avard-Dixon Building (renovation, 1994)

Central heating plant (renovation, 1994)

"Glasshouse" / Greenhouse (2001)

B. BURTT BARTEAUX & ASSOCIATES

Hunton House (renovation, 1981)

Bennett House (renovation, 1982)

Bigelow House (renovation, 1982)

DOUGLAS BROWN ARCHITECT

Harold Crabtree Building (1980)

BROWN, BRISLEY & BROWN

Mount Allison Chapel (1965)

Gairdner Fine Arts Building (1965)

Marjorie Young Bell Conservatory of Music (1966)

Chemistry building [Barclay Chemistry Building] (co-designers, 1967)

Edwards House (1969)

Thornton House (1969)

Ralph Pickard Bell Library (1970)

University Student Centre (renovation, 1971)

Owens Art Gallery (co-designers of renovation, 1972)

SAMUEL C. BUGBEE

Mount Allison Wesleyan Academy [First male academy building] (1843)

CECIL BURGESS

Allison Gardens (1948)

EDMUND BURKE

Owens Art Gallery (1895)

Hammond House [President's House] (1897)

Borden Hall (1904)

BURKE & HORWOOD

Second (men's) university residence (1900)

Jairus Hart Hall (1910; addition, 1920)

REV. GEORGE BUTCHER

Mount Allison Male Academy [Second male academy building] (1867)

ANDREW COBB

Memorial Library (1927)

Science building [Flemington Science Building] (co-designers, 1931)

Centennial Hall (renovation, 1934)

COMBE & RYAN

Science building [Flemington Science Building] (co-designers, 1931)

GUSTAVO DA ROZA

Owens Art Gallery (co-designers of renovation, 1972)

DUFFUS, ROMANS, SINGLE & KUNDZINS

Chemistry building [Barclay Chemistry Building] (co-designers, 1967)

JAMES C. DUMARESQ

First (men's) university residence (1894)

ROBERT EATON

Bermuda House (renovation, 1985)

G. ERNEST FAIRWEATHER

Centennial Memorial Hall (1883)

Mount Allison Male Academy [Third male academy building] (1883)

Conservatory of Music (1891)

FEDERAL DEPARTMENT OF PUBLIC WORKS

Animal Pathology Building [Bennett Building] (1956)

FENCO (FOUNDATION OF CANADA ENGINEERING CORPORATION LIMITED)

Athletic Centre (co-designers, 1961)

Marjorie Young Bell Convocation Hall (1966)

C.A. FOWLER & COMPANY

"Temporary" gym (1921)

Central Heating Plant (1931)

Mount Allison Academy [Fourth male academy building; Palmer Hall] (1934)

Trueman House (1946)

Tweedie Hall (1946)

Physics and Engineering Building [PEG Building] (1958)

Avard-Dixon Building (1959)

Bennett House (1959)

Bigelow House (1959)

Hunton House (1959)

William Morley Tweedie Annex [Memorial Library addition] (1960)

McConnell Hall (1963)

WILLARD M. MITCHELL

Charles Fawcett Memorial Hall (1910)

SPERRY & PARTNERS

Campbell Hall (2004)

Harper Hall (renovation, 2004)

Wallace McCain Student Centre (renovation, 2008)

SPROATT & ROLPH

Athletic Centre (co-designers, 1961)

GARNET W. WILSON

Normandy Hall (1947)

Ortona Hall (1947)

ZEIDLER PARTNERSHIP

Purdy Crawford Centre for the Arts (2014)

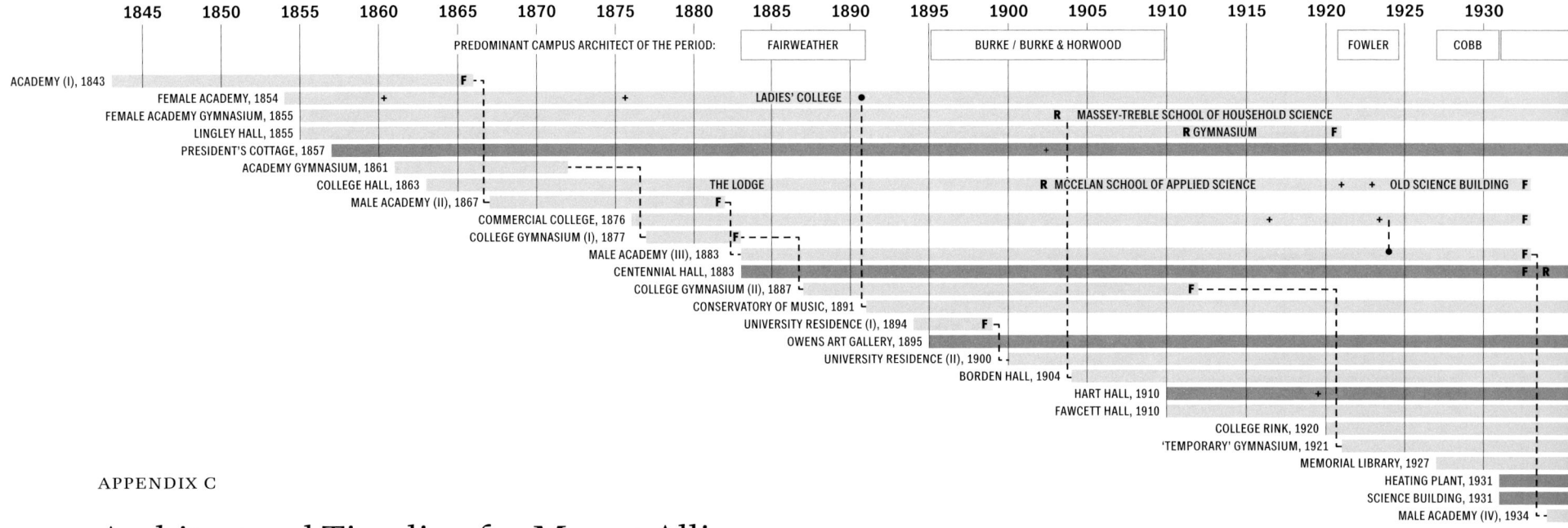

APPENDIX C

Architectural Timeline for Mount Allison

	Building exists
	Building no longer exists
IIII	Period of building's existence before purchase by university
F	Building consumed by fire
D	Building demolished
R	Building substantially renovated
S	Building sold
+	Building enlarged
--•-	Addition connected to building
⌐-⌐	Building's function transferred to a new building

SATELLITE HOUSES: Other buildings not depicted on the time line which were at one time owned by Mount Allison include: Cuthbertson House (84 York); German House (123 York); MacGregor House (124 York); 38, 42, 84, 85, 87 & 89 York; Sprague House (15 Salem); Baxter House (17 Salem); French House (31–31A Salem); and Pavillion Bousquet (57 Charlotte). The university also occupied two local hotels as temporary residences: The Brunswick Hotel (1941–59) and The Ford Hotel (renamed Allison Hall, 1920–52).

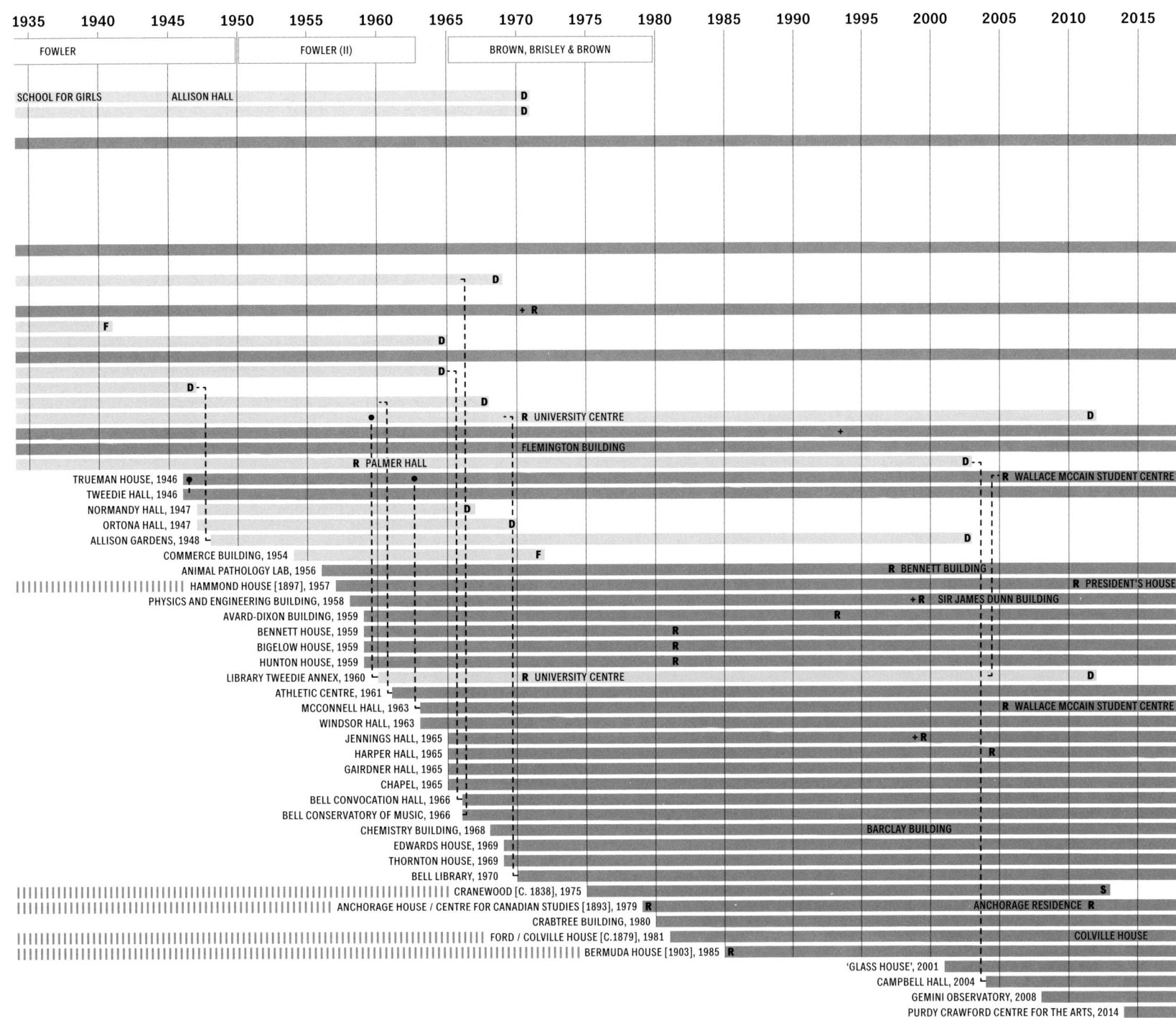

1935　1940　1945　1950　1955　1960　1965　1970　1975　1980　1985　1990　1995　2000　2005　2010　2015

FOWLER　　　FOWLER (II)　　　BROWN, BRISLEY & BROWN

SCHOOL FOR GIRLS　　ALLISON HALL　　　　D
　　　　　　　　　　　　　　　　　　　　D

　　　　　　　　　　　　　　　　　　D

　　　　　　　　　　　　　　　　+ R

F

　　　　　　　　　　　　　　D

　　　　　　　　　　　　D

　　D

　　　　　　　　D

　　　　　　　　　　　R UNIVERSITY CENTRE　　　　　　　　　　　　　　D
　　　　　　　　　　　　　　　　　　　+
　　　　　　　　　FLEMINGTON BUILDING
　　　　　　　　　　　　　　　　　　　　　　　D
R PALMER HALL　　　　　　　　　　　　R WALLACE MCCAIN STUDENT CENTRE
TRUEMAN HOUSE, 1946
TWEEDIE HALL, 1946
NORMANDY HALL, 1947　　　　　D
ORTONA HALL, 1947　　　　　　D
ALLISON GARDENS, 1948　　　　　　　　　　　　　　　　　　　　D
COMMERCE BUILDING, 1954　　　F
ANIMAL PATHOLOGY LAB, 1956　　　　　　　　　　　R BENNETT BUILDING
HAMMOND HOUSE [1897], 1957　　　　　　　　　　　　　　　　R PRESIDENT'S HOUSE
PHYSICS AND ENGINEERING BUILDING, 1958　　+ R　SIR JAMES DUNN BUILDING
AVARD-DIXON BUILDING, 1959　　　　　　　R
BENNETT HOUSE, 1959　　　R
BIGELOW HOUSE, 1959　　　R
HUNTON HOUSE, 1959　　　R
LIBRARY TWEEDIE ANNEX, 1960　　　R UNIVERSITY CENTRE　　　　　　　D
ATHLETIC CENTRE, 1961
MCCONNELL HALL, 1963　　　　　　　　　　　　R WALLACE MCCAIN STUDENT CENTRE
WINDSOR HALL, 1963
JENNINGS HALL, 1965　　　　　　　+ R
HARPER HALL, 1965　　　　　　　　R
GAIRDNER HALL, 1965
CHAPEL, 1965
BELL CONVOCATION HALL, 1966
BELL CONSERVATORY OF MUSIC, 1966
CHEMISTRY BUILDING, 1968　　　　BARCLAY BUILDING
EDWARDS HOUSE, 1969
THORNTON HOUSE, 1969
BELL LIBRARY, 1970
CRANEWOOD [C. 1838], 1975　　　　　　　　　　S
ANCHORAGE HOUSE / CENTRE FOR CANADIAN STUDIES [1893], 1979 R　　ANCHORAGE RESIDENCE R
CRABTREE BUILDING, 1980
FORD / COLVILLE HOUSE [C.1879], 1981　　　　　COLVILLE HOUSE
BERMUDA HOUSE [1903], 1985 R
'GLASS HOUSE', 2001
CAMPBELL HALL, 2004
GEMINI OBSERVATORY, 2008
PURDY CRAWFORD CENTRE FOR THE ARTS, 2014

About the Contributors

Architect and art historian JOHN LEROUX takes a holistic view of his profession, seeing beyond buildings themselves into the cultural, intellectual and physical landscapes to which they contribute. Leroux graduated from the McGill School of Architecture in 1994 and completed a master's degree in Canadian Art History at Concordia University in 2002. He has worked at several award-winning architecture firms in Toronto, Atlanta and New Brunswick, and also teaches at the University of New Brunswick, where he is concurrently pursuing doctoral studies in cultural history. He has won many awards for architectural and public art projects throughout Canada, and has pursued various creative disciplines, such as set design for Theatre New Brunswick. In 2012, he was a team member selected to take part in Canada's official entry at the 2012 Venice Biennale in Architecture. A contributing architecture columnist for the *Telegraph-Journal* and *Canadian Architect*, he is also the author of six books on New Brunswick architecture, including *Building New Brunswick*, *St. Andrews Architecture: 1604–1966* and most recently *Glorious Light: The Stained Glass of Fredericton*.

THADDEUS HOLOWNIA's photographs have been the subject of numerous exhibitions, including most recently, *Paris after Atget* at the Corkin Gallery in Toronto, *Working in the Dark: An Homage to John Thompson* at Galerie 12 in Moncton, *Thaddeus Holownia: The Terra Nova Suite*, a twenty-five-year survey of his work in Newfoundland & Labrador organized by the Provincial Art Gallery (the ROOMS) in St. John's Newfoundland. His 1998 solo exhibition, *Extended Vision: Photographs by Thaddeus Holownia 1978–1997*—a mid-career retrospective organized by the Canadian Museum of Contemporary Photography—travelled across Canada and to the Centro de la Imagen in Mexico City. In 2000 Holownia was elected to the Royal Canadian Academy of Arts. He received a Fulbright Fellowship in 2001 and the Paul Paré Medal in 1998 and 2006 from Mount Allison University in recognition of excellence in teaching, creative activity, research and community service. In 2015 he was honoured with the Lieutenant Governor of New Brunswick's Award for Excellence in the Visual Arts and the Order of New Brunswick.

233

Acknowledgements & Sources

We thank our partners, Meghan Leroux and Gay Hansen. We would also like to gratefully acknowledge Mount Allison archivist David Mawhinney and the New Brunswick Arts Board for their generous support of this project. Likewise, we also want to thank the following individuals: Allen Bentley, Lesley Bonang, Douglas & Gwen Brown, Jamie Burke, Herménégilde Chiasson, The Clares Studio, Ian Colford, Gary Dunfield, Tarek El-Khatib, Michael Fox, Charles A.E. Fowler, Julie Fracker, David Frank, Linda Fraser, Rice Fuller, Trish Goguen, Patrick Griffin, Theo Holownia, Christie Lawrence, Beth Leroux, Conrad Leroux, Gary Leroux, Rod McDonald, Steve Mannell, Heath Matheson, Mike Meade, Charles "Scoop" Moffatt, Lucy O'Sullivan, Martin Patriquin, Mark Payne, Pridham Studios, John G. Reid, Bob Roberts, Sylvia Rowan, Garry Shutlak, Andrew Steeves, Donna Sullivan, Jane Tisdale, the University of New Brunswick's history department, and James Wilson.

Text sources have been credited in the sidenotes while image sources have been listed on the facing page. All uncredited images are by Thaddeus Holownia. The following abbreviations are used to identify archival collections:

BANC—Bancroft Library, University of California (Berkeley, CF)
CAA—Canadian Architectural Archives, University of Calgary (Calgary, AB)
MCA—Maritime Conference Archives, United Church of Canada (Halifax, NS)
MAA—Mount Allison University Archives (Sackville, NB)
NSA—Nova Scotia Archives (Halifax, NS)
PANB—Provincial Archives of New Brunswick (Fredericton, NB)
WMMS—Wesleyan Methodist Missionary Society Archives (London, ON)
UNBASC—University of New Brunswick, Archives & Special Collections (Fredericton, NB)

Typically, photo captions provide information in the following order: name of the building, name of the architect or architectural firm (if applicable) and the year construction was completed on the project.

234

IMAGE SOURCES

[Pages 6–7] MAA, 2007.07.1167.
1.2 PANB, MC1236–530–6
1.3 BANC, BANC PIC 1905.17500.10:261
1.4 MAA, 2007.07.583
1.5 MAA, 2007.07.1193
1.6 MAA 2007.07.128
1.7 MAA, 2007.07.1206
1.8 MAA 2007.07.838
1.9 MAA, 2007.07.916
1.10 MAA, 2007.07.1438
2.1 MAA, *The Mount Allison Institutions*
2.3 MAA, 2007.07.163
2.4 MAA, 2007.07.1193
2.5 MAA, 2007.07.1021
2.6 MAA, 2007.07.164
2.7 MAA, 2007.07.266
2.8 MAA, 2007.07.278
2.9 MAA, 2007.07.267
2.10 MAA 2007.07.269
2.11 MAA, 2007.07.34
2.12 MAA, 2007.07.708
2.13 Harvey Studios, Fredericton
2.14 MAA, 2007.07.45
2.15 Collection of Thaddeus Holownia
2.16 MAA, 2007.07.657
2.17 MAA, 5501.9.2.1.64
2.18 MAA, 5501.9.2.4.8
2.20 MAA, 5501.9.2.1.22
2.24 MAA, 2007.07.1472
2.25 MAA, 2007.07.1488
2.26 MAA, 2007.07.59
3.1 MAA, 2007.07.953
3.2 Collection of Thaddeus Holownia
3.3 MAA, 2007.07.964
3.4 MAA, 2007.07.1024
3.5 MAA, 2007.07.122
3.6 MAA, 2007.07.332
3.7 MAA, 2007.07.1397
3.8 MAA, 2007.07.1399
3.9 Collection of Thaddeus Holownia
3.10 MAA, 2007.07.771
3.11 MAA, *The Argosy* (December 1912), p. 157a
3.12 MAA, 2007.07.831

3.15 MAA, *Mount Allison Ladies' College Calendar 1929–30*
3.16 MAA, 8916.1.9
3.17 MAA, AR2-8665 Old Gymnasium
3.19 Collection of Thaddeus Holownia
3.20 MAA, 2007.07.876
3.21 MAA, 2006.01.2.4, *Mount Allison is Yours*, pp. 8, 10, 12
3.22 MAA, 2006.01.2.4, *Mount Allison is Yours*, p. 6
3.23 Collection of Thaddeus Holownia
3.25 MAA, 2007.07.800
3.27 MAA, 2007.07.263
3.28 MAA, 2007.07.712
3.29 NSA, 2.3.16.11
3.30 MAA, 8675/AR1/Sketch of Proposed Layout for Mt. Allison Academy [1933]
3.31 Collection of Thaddeus Holownia
3.32 Collection of Thaddeus Holownia
3.35 MAA, 2007.07.715
3.37 MAA, 2007.07.962
4.1 MAA, 8665/AR2/Proposed Student Residences file 1
4.2 MAA, 2007.07.366
4.4 MAA, 2007.07.346
4.5 MAA, 2007.07.350
4.6 Collection of Thaddeus Holownia
4.7 Collection of Thaddeus Holownia
4.8 Collection of Thaddeus Holownia
4.9 Donna L. Sullivan
4.11 MAA, 2007.07.1462
4.12 MAA, 2007.07.1463
4.13 MAA, 2007.07.1464
4.14 MAA, 2007.07.724
4.15 MAA, 2007.07.627
4.17 MAA, 8665/AR2/University Centre file
4.18 MAA, 2007.07.891
4.19 MAA, 2007.07.866
4.20 MAA, 2007.07.1458
4.21 MAA, 2007.07.1450
4.22 MAA, 2007.07.601
4.23 MAA, 2007.07.613
4.24 MAA, 2007.07.762

4.25 MAA, 2007.07.1493
4.26 MAA, 8805/5
4.27 MAA, 2007.07.1490
4.28 MAA, 2007.07.816
4.29 MAA, 2007.07.830
4.30 MAA, 2007.07.347
5.1 CAA, Panda Associates fonds, PAN 60945
5.2 CAA, Panda Associates fonds, PAN 60945
5.3 MAA, 2007.07.1475
5.4 MAA, 2007.07.1476
5.5 MAA, 8665/AR1/Chapel file 2/1
5.6 MAA, 8665/AR1/Chapel file 1
5.7 UNBASC, UA RG 329, box 19, file 14
5.8 MAA, 2007.07.748
5.9 MAA, 2007.07.970
5.10 MAA, 8665/AR1/Chapel file 9/1
5.11 MAA, 2007.07.752
5.17 MAA, 2007.07.510
5.18 MAA, 2007.07.811
5.19 MAA, 2007.07.812
5.20 MAA, 8665/AR2/Marjorie Young Bell Conservatory of Music file
5.23 MAA, 8665/AR2/Marjorie Young Bell Conservatory of Music file
5.24 MAA, 2007.07.1454
5.28 MAA, 2008.55/20
5.30 MAA, 2007.07.1457
5.31 MAA, 8665/AR2/Proposed Student Residences file
5.34 MAA, 2007.07.1495
5.35 MAA, 2007.07.323
5.39 MAA, CR1-7001/240 Surveys of the Isthmus of Chignecto
5.40 MAA, 2007.07.701
5.42 Cranbrook Academy of Art, Michigan

This book was designed and typeset by Andrew Steeves at Gaspereau Press. The typefaces are Rod McDonald's Goluska & Classic Grotesque.

7   6   5   4   3   2   1

LIBRARY AND ARCHIVES CANADA CATALOGUING IN PUBLICATION

Leroux, John, 1970–, author
A vision in wood & stone : the architecture of Mount
Allison University / John Leroux & Thaddeus Holownia.

Includes bibliographical references and index.
ISBN 978-1-55447-140-9 (bound)

1. Mount Allison University—Buildings—History.   2. College buildings—New Brunswick—Sackville—History.   3. Architecture—New Brunswick—Sackville—History.   4. Sackville (N.B.)—Buildings, structures, etc.
I. Holownia, Thaddeus, 1949–, photographer   II. Title.

LE3.M92L47 2016   727'.30971523   C2016-900754-5

GASPEREAU PRESS LIMITED ¶ GARY DUNFIELD
& ANDREW STEEVES ¶ PRINTERS & PUBLISHERS
47 Church Avenue, Kentville, Nova Scotia B4N 2M7
Literary Outfitters & Cultural Wilderness Guides

Canada   NOVA SCOTIA